LIFE 2.0

SAMRAT BERA

ISBN 13: 978-1-945532-23-8

Published and Edited by Opportune Independent Publishing Company

Printed in the United States of America

For permission requests, write to the publisher, addressed "Attention: Permissions Coordinator" to the address below.

info@opportunepublishing.com

www. opportunepublishing.com

DISCLAIMER

This book is not meant to offend or go against any person, group, religion or institution, nor is it meant to show one above the other. These are just my own opinions which may, or may not, be accurate.

TABLE OF CONTENTS

FOREWORD
& THANK YOU

First, I would like to thank my loving wife for encouraging me to write this book, the second person to inspire me to write after my father. I would also like to thank my parents for having brought me up very open to different ideas and faiths and seeing the world with a very non-biased approach. For the countless discussions, we have had, especially over dinner on the purpose of life and life after death.

Like many folks, I too have thought pensively on life—why was I born, was I meant to do something, am I realizing that or is the material world keeping me involved so much, that I am unable to see the real and obvious? Is technology and advances in science that we are making have any connection with our scriptures?

Science and Spirituality–what have we been taught and what do we believe? Are they essentially two sides of the same coin or are they diametrically opposite to each other?

I could have written this book earlier, but it was not meant to be. Just like a flower blooms only at a given time of the year, I too had that urge to pen my thoughts down and share with you all my thoughts on this topic and at this moment in my life.

This is a synopsis of the world as I see it and my ideas and thoughts of how this universe operates. I just felt that I should share my thoughts with a larger audience at this time as this was meant to be.

I would like to acknowledge and attribute this book to my daughter, who at such a young age, has started appreciating and understanding the bigger picture and who is the source of so much happiness in my life—she has made me complete.

Above all, I thank God who has given me the strength and the resolve to try to pen my thoughts down. Without Him, the entire journey would have been implausible, very empty and hollow. I thank Him for trying to make me understand my place in this universe and allowing me to bring my thoughts to the world.

In this book, I have tried to capture the ethos of the many spiritual masters and their gospels, our holy scriptures and their teachings, the way science and technology are evolving, my self-assessment to life and who we are as people while trying to make sense of it all.

These are my thoughts and assumptions only and are not a representation from any other party, person or company.

Some of the concepts may be extremely complex to understand and in the same vein, can be very, very, simple! It is simple themes that are governed by very strict and strong cosmic rules without which chaos and lawlessness would abound.

The journey called life is beautiful and knowing the meaning of it all makes it not only beautiful but very meaningful as well!

This work is to try to bring out the meaning of our existence, answer some questions that we might have and give some definition to this scenic journey called life or should we say a part of the human evolution—Life 2.0!

CHAPTER ONE

SAVING MY DAUGHTER

A rocket bomb exploded next to my daughter —Jia's car. Zig-Zig-Zig–the shots pelted Jia's passenger side door, and she swerved hard to take the road out of the city and into the mountains. I followed in hot pursuit, but so did the enemy!

My mind was racing with thoughts and questions- What had Jia done wrong? How did she get into this situation? Had she fallen into bad company or had she stumbled on to some secret? Was she running with money, information or something else? Who was she running from? Is she on the good or bad side? Why was she being followed?

My mind started getting fuzzy with all these thoughts and my stomach wrenched at the sound of those gunshots. Was there a deficiency in the way we had brought Jia up?

She was an intelligent and hard-working "next door" type of girl—just finished her degree in engineering and landed her first job. We've never met any suspicious friends of hers, and she's never been into drugs or anything like that… so what was going on?

The only way to find out was to keep following her and try to get her out of this current mess!

As Jia sped away from the city and up a slope, there came a fork in the road. She took a right turn, and all our cars sped up, following as closely behind as possible. With every turn and move, I saw parts of the upcoming city building up in front of my eyes. With every mile, I could see more of the city's downtown, as well as the countryside hills coming into view as we sped down the roads.

What was most shocking, yet pleasing to me was

the fact that Jia had a car which had guns spitting out bullets and laser toward the enemy cars.

Was I dreaming? This was not a James Bond or Mission Impossible movie; this was real! I quickly snapped back into reality. By then, Jia had got into a desolate part of the city and parked her car behind an old dilapidated building.

This place looked something like the ruins of a fort, but I knew why she had stopped there. There were many levels, doors, stairs, alleys and places where you could hide and fight. Maybe she had an accomplice, or help, available there.

The enemy cars—there were three of them–slowly circled the fort, they began to get out and take cover in a covert military style operation. I thought to myself, *Should I call the police? Were these Secret Service agents, drug smugglers, the Mafia or foreign agents*? I couldn't call the police unless I knew exactly what was going on.

So, I drew my gun and put on my night vision glasses. I saw there were 3 to 4 people in each car, so there must have been 9 to 12 people in all that my daughter and I would need to handle. I did not want to risk calling Jia on her phone, as the sound of her ringtone or the light from her cellphone's screen could give her away.

So, I began the attack on my own. I put a silencer on my gun, aimed for the last man standing and took him down. Less than a second later, I saw that the first guy had reached Jia up on the second floor. In the blink of an eye, they were locked in a hand fight, and they were fighting hard. Being a black belt in Taekwondo, my daughter was doing well for herself.

But, suddenly things turned-this burly man pinned her down and had a deathlike grip on her neck. I felt sick and helpless and started praying to God. Thankfully at that very moment, Jia hit him on his chin with her elbow, jerking his head upward and gave one swift kick to the middle of his neck, hitting his Adam's apple.

He was motionless after that and fell in a heap. I gloated with glee and started to think of how I could do my part to save my daughter and get both of us out of this mess.

As I started looking around with my telescopic lens fitted to my machine gun, I saw something that I could have never imagined and had only read about in fantasy and fiction novels. The guy I had just taken down—I could've sworn my bullet had gone through his head–as well as the burly guy who my daughter had killed on the second floor, both got up and started walking.

It seemed impossible, but they had spawned themselves! This was going to be an extremely long and impossible night, with an even longer death defying fight! How could we fight an invincible force that can heal itself and get up again?

At this point, my mind was racing all over the place. Was this some alien force? Had Jia visited the US Defense and Innovation centers, or Area 51, and stumbled on some secret project? How on Earth would my daughter and I survive a legion as supreme and powerful as this?

Hohl, Call of Duty 2015

However, there was no other way around it; I just had to go on and do whatever it took to save my daughter! I trod on carefully trying to see any silhouettes, figures or any lurking shadows, but I couldn't see any. The clouds weren't helping either, as the only light was that of the half-moon in the sky.

Suddenly, I heard a cry—it came from a woman nearby. She fell flat on her back and laid motionless. I knew it wasn't my daughter; this lady had long blonde hair and was bigger than my daughter.

I decided to try and find out what exactly was going on, even though I knew this was putting both our lives in danger. With my daughter up there fighting alone with this group, or species I wasn't aware of, I needed to know what we were up against.

As I neared the lady, I saw that she had been shot somewhere between her chest and solar plexus writhing in agony and pain. But oddly enough, she wasn't bleeding. She was trying to reach for her belt. It was a weird belt—not leather, cloth or anything I had seen before. It seemed to be made of metal with a red button in the middle. She was trying to reach for that button, and she finally did.

The very moment she did, she stopped quivering, and her whole body jolted as if she were struck by lightning. Her pale face became clear and fresh, and her eyes went from being shut to being wide open, and she gave me a silver and steely gaze.

Fearing the assault and onslaught that would follow, I quickly raised my weapon and fired all the shots I had in my magazine straight towards her body. All she did was raise her hand with her palm pointing towards me, and my bullets just fell in front of her. I realized she had created some sort of a defense shield around her that my bullets could not penetrate.

Then, she looked at me hard, and fire emanated from her eyes, engulfing me in flames in just seconds. It was scorching! As I grappled with my plight and situation, all thoughts of fighting and my daughter disappeared from my mind. I tried rolling on the tarmac, trying to douse the flames on my body. As I rolled, my daughter jumped from the balcony above and took position between this woman and I. What followed next was just like a sci-fi movie! A fight ensued between both the women, one upstaging the other. Then something that had me cringe with fear and amazement happened—My daughter took out a rod from which there was a beam of light emanating from both ends—I realized what she had in her hands was a laser sword!

She wielded it expertly and started attacking her opponent. Before long, more of the enemy had arrived; some were jumping from the higher floors, while others suddenly emerged from the shadows of the walls.

We were outnumbered! Within seconds, the others closed in on my daughter. I exchanged glances with Jia for the first time. My glance clearly asked a lot of questions, and hers gave a lot of answers, but we both ended up asking the same question in that gaze —"What are you doing here?"

But, it didn't matter—we were here, and we had to fight. There was simply no other option. Jia raised her sword and started attacking the enemy. They jumped up, dodging her laser sword. I was trying to shoot at them but realized what a futile exercise this was. These folks would dodge the bullets, move at lightning speed and in the rare case they were hit, they would respawn themselves. These guys could take down an entire nation's army all by themselves. They were a race so supreme and advanced that no science and technology available today could bring them down. The beloved human race was done for, or so I thought.

As I watched the fight unfold before me, the meaning of God Almighty started taking on an entirely new meaning in my mind. The meaning of life started changing for me. We already know there is a beginning and an end to everything. But, what if you could just respawn yourself and never die? What if there is another life out there that is more superior to us?

Several questions that had been going on in my mind for so many years started gripping me even more than usual. Questions like: Why do we have to die? If we are born by God Almighty's grace, why is the end so painful for the person dying, as well as for that person's loved ones? Why do plants have fruits and flowers only at certain times and why do they wither and die?

Why do all these have to come to an end, and in most cases, in the most unpleasant way—death by old age, disease, accident and so on and so forth? Very few people are fortunate enough to die while sleeping or instantly without realization. I am happy with my life, but I am afraid of what happens next.

To be frank, I am not sure where I will end up and the uncertainty that I will be plagued with–what kind of conditions, people and place would I be in? Gosh, questions and questions galore, but no answers!

As these thoughts started going through my mind, I heard my beloved wife's voice calling out to our daughter and I, "Come down guys, dinner is ready." Jia and I took off our virtual reality glasses, stopped the video game and walked down to the dining room.

On the way, my daughter mentioned she wanted to

play tennis on the game box after dinner, as she was saturated playing the other game and needed an easier and less taxing game. I kept thinking, *could I change the game by just replacing the character from playing the soldier trying to fight to that of a tennis player or a car racer depending on my will and thought? Or, could I be transported into another setting and be given the experience of that scene after being fed different inputs and a change of settings? Could life just be a game and merely a different context we are put into?"*

My mind was spinning coming out from playing that game, from the possibilities and unexplainable thoughts going on in my head. I barely heard my wife asking me if the food was good. My daughter giggled away as I stared into nothingness–deep and pensive of what I had just realized!

Are we also playing a game, or enacting it? Is the time warp and time portal for real? Can we transport ourselves from one location context to another? How was all of this working in a pragmatic way that could be understood and that made sense?

Is there a meaning to everything happening after all? Are we just not there yet and not prepared to understand what is going on? Or, is this all just a figment of imagination and merely a different perspective?

We have seen some of the things from the past becoming a reality in the future. If you told someone 100 years ago, that Tom Brady would be playing football in Houston, TX and that people from around the world would be able to watch the game live, it would have been called far-fetched and impossible. But lo–came the era of Television and cable TV and changed all that.

The same goes for other spheres of our lives. Be it cell phones and being accessible on the go, being able to detect and predict using video analytics or running unmanned vehicles in the far-flung areas of the universe. Many things thought unattainable can become a reality in just a generation.

Is it possible that the technological evolutions we see now, and in the future, will transcend boundaries that exist between the supernatural and us? Is it possible that one day we will come to an inflection point where there will be so much that we have achieved and learned, that the difference between Man and God takes an altogether new meaning?

But what about the scriptures, beliefs and thoughts handed down to us from previous generations? Who do we feel is the right person, or path, to follow? Is there a way that all the paths, beliefs, science and technology somehow, somewhere come together?

They must because one cannot be exclusive of the other. Or, are they mutually exclusive and can both schools of thoughts—one on scriptures and beliefs and the other on science and facts–coexist together?

All I will say at this stage is to take a deep breath and explore the different facets of the world around us. Sure, there are things that we know for certain, some we know a little about and many things we have no idea about.

But, looking at each of them in a calm and objective manner will dispel some of those thoughts that go against our belief systems and create more thoughts that will raise further questions.

And that is the way it is meant to be!

Chris, Sder 2012

CHAPTER TWO

———————◦◦———————

OUR HOLY SCRIPTURES

L et us take a quick segway into what our holy scriptures say. I have read some religious scriptures like the Bible, Gita, Quran, Buddhist scriptures and I have come to an understanding that the basic tenets of what they teach us are quite similar:

1. *Be good and do good to your family, friends, neighbors, society and others.*

2. *Share a part of your earnings with the poor and needy.*

3. *Always believe and thank God Almighty for everything–your life, food, shelter, profession*

and other folks or things attached to oneself.

4. *Be truthful and support the truth–don't lie, be deceitful or cheat.*

5. *Spread love.*

6. *Don't harm, hurt or kill anyone or anybody's feelings and emotions.*

7. *Pray and remember the Lord/God/Almighty always.*

8. *Observe some days of penance, fasting and abstinence.*

Most of our scriptures make one aware that the Lord is watching and that you must settle your account/score when you go up to the Heavens, or a place where you are to be in your afterlife. Hence, the higher you score on the above points, the easier it will be to gain access to God's Heavenly abode.

The more you digress from the teachings or the cardinal rules, the tougher it will be for you. Whether it's the Ten Commandments or the main points in Buddhism, Hinduism, Islam or the other religions, all of them allude to the same and basic tenets of conducting one's life—to be righteous and strong. None of them ever says to take a life, harm or cheat someone for your benefit.

There are different mythological stories written to make us understand these teachings and sayings in a common and easily understood language. Based on the way we conduct our lives, our thoughts and actions have a strong correlation to our afterlife in the heavens, or in hell.

Some of our faiths and religions go further and define in varying detail about the concept of the Soul and what happens to it when we die. As well as how the Soul is created and the journey it takes— we will explore more about this in the next chapter.

We go to our churches, mosques, synagogues, temples and other places of worship and have our own understanding and beliefs about God, life and the path to the heavenly abode and why we should aspire to reach there. So many books have been written on this topic—from an angle of religion,

Photographed by William Blake

philosophy, faiths and our celestial journey. But, what is so different about *Life 2.0*?

Most of us have been exposed to and understand the meaning of life, the existence of God and the meaning of living happily with one another. We may think only a very small percentage of people are unaware of this, but on the contrary, a large percentage of us are not aware of the things taught by other faiths or what other religions profess.

Sadly, some even feel that other religions are inferior to theirs.

This has resulted in unnecessary misunderstandings, battles, fights, extremism and barbaric activities that we see in today's world. We are so dogmatized by our beliefs that we fail to see outside of what we are exposed to by our religious leaders. While some of the spiritual and religious leaders are exemplary, there are some who cannot be spoken highly of at all.

Time and time again, we find instances of some religious leader or someone in that organization sexually abusing men, women and children—this comes up time and again in different religions and different parts of the world.

We also have instances where these leaders manipulate one's mind by giving their followers incorrect information and making them accept it.

Children and many other innocent souls are like clay; you can shape a person's mind using your teachings and direction—be it right, or wrong. The child grows up believing what has been taught and considers that to be the truth.

During the adult life, some children commit crimes, but they do it not knowing what they are doing as they have been brainwashed from childhood. Which is the reason, why we as good citizens, teachers, friends, parents and family have a moral duty to imbibe the right values in our children and next generations. And those values need to be global, all-encompassing and teach love and togetherness not hate towards another or be regionalized in the thoughts.

The wider the perspective, the more we can give and derive from one another.

I feel whenever we are setting out to harm someone, a place or thing, we should just ask ourselves and our conscience:

1. *Did God want us to unite or divide?*

2. *Did He want us to fight each other and take lives, treasure and kingdoms, or did He want us to live peacefully with one another?*

3. *Did He want us to spread hate and fear, or spread love and compassion?*

4. *Did He want us to end one another, or support each other to advance our species into the world of tomorrow?*

5. *Did He want us to create bombs and ruin the planet and the solar system, or did He want us to create better places for us and for our future generations to live?*

6. Most importantly, did God create religion?

If we were to believe that it was not God who created religion, then why do we have so many religions? Why do we have so many people fighting against each other in the name of their religion? Why do we not worship that one God who we feel is the most supreme of them all?

Does that mean there are many Gods as well as different Kingdoms of Gods, or is there truth in the scriptures that there is only one God? In which case, what are we fighting for and for what reason and to achieve what objective, if we are finally sons and daughters of the same God?

It does not matter what religion or faith anyone follows, we must remember that the Lord (most of us have that in common) created the World, the universe, the galaxies, the solar systems, and the planets and the stars, but He did not create religion! Similarly, he did not create countries; we did–all for a reason! But the reason is being misinterpreted and hence causing pain and suffering.

Let us leave the entire universe and its grandness and take just our small planet–Earth. The Lord created this beautiful world for us. No one is blind to the things He has created to help support a species like us—it's a work of exemplary engineering!

He created the human body, which has lungs and needs air to breathe and survive. It needs oxygen to burn our food inside our stomach, and He created the atmosphere with air and oxygen in it. We needed food to live, and He created plants with fruits and vegetables for us to live on. We needed more of our kind, and He created the reproductive system in us so that we can produce more of us.

He created man and woman so that this procreation is enabled further, and He did that for all the other species. He also created different animals, plants and flowers and other beautiful things to make us happy and entertained.

For our existence, He did one of the most important things—He spun the planet around so that it rotates. This process is what gives us day and night so that we all can do work during the day and after getting tired, we can go to sleep and rest at night. The rotation also creates wind patterns that help the clouds to move from one part of the world to another and bring rain–such a wonderful and automatic system to transport water.

He even tilted the Earth's axis to enable these atmospheric flows to spread air and natural masses —snow, rain, streams, etc. This is the reason why we have seasons; if the Earth were on a straight axis, we would all have had the same temperature conditions throughout the year. He created this so that we have a variety in life and see different manifestations of flowers, temperatures and seasons.

Isn't it clear why we need to acknowledge what the Creator has given us and thank the Creator for the same? I marvel at the creation from every angle. A simple case in point—we try to make canals and struggle when there is a mountain or chasm to go through, but clouds don't have such problems.

That is one of the solutions the Creator has provided to bring rain from the bodies of water to the other far flung areas in land. One who is oblivious to all this grandeur perhaps has a disturbed mind which is muddled with some or the other craving or problems clouding their mind. There are different ways to change this person—spiritual healing, meditation and other techniques can help.

I feel while we do these, you will not be able to change everyone, as it was just not meant to be! Not all were meant to understand or appreciate the grandeur or be at peace with all the problems plaguing our lives.

As we go on this journey, we will explore another part of our lives where we have no control, and we know not why we see, hear or endure certain things, people, events or situations. But we will see why things happen in a certain manner and what can and should we do to tackle those situations.

At one point in time, per our scientific community, we only had one big landmass (in some theories like that of Wegener's and the continental drift theory), there were a few land crusts on the Earth's mantle which came together and with the rotation, the landmasses kept moving further apart which led to the creation of our continents. In time, all the landmasses will come together again. It will be a few million, maybe a billion years before this happens.

But once you start understanding the larger laws at play, the meaning of life will be slowly and better understood. We, just like the Earth, continents and the tectonic plates, are created, shifted and moved around. We all also have a natural end but will resurface again. Thus, the cycle of birth and death will continue.

The Lord created the Moon to give the gravitational pull to create the waves and the water streams–convection, conduction, evaporation, condensation and other laws that help us. Unfortunately, He also created self-destructing laws that give birth to earthquakes, tsunamis and other powerful natural forces.

But, these are just self-healing and self-correcting events for the existence of our planet and the larger good. He created the Sun to give light and warmth to keep us and all the vegetation, plant and animal life

Ostow, 2012, Discovery

alive and healthy. He also created the phenomena of death and self-destruction. Once we understand the big picture, we will also understand why that is good and needed as well.

The human body itself is a work of supreme art– the way we breathe, consume food, reproduce, and take out toxic substances from our body. The way we grow from conception to passing away, our senses and our emotions—plus the interactions and experiences we have and the billions of stories that each one of us generates—it is magnificent!

Do you see what I am getting at? All the things around us and our world including ourselves are being governed by strong scientific laws–some of which we understand today and many of which we don't. We will speak about this in a different perspective later but let us hold on to the thought —and marvel at the grand creation!

While the Creator has created all this grandeur, it is worth introspecting on what we have created. On one hand, we have created and derived enormous benefits from science and technology. Every sphere of our lives has been touched and changed for the better and has been a boon, but on the other hand, we are also the creators of some of the very problems that plague us today.

While I feel a few examples of the things created by us were for our good, I feel many of those same examples have been misinterpreted over a period and been leveraged for personal gains. The main three that I feel has robbed us of our peace of mind and body and created huge sufferings are:

1. *Religion*

2. *Countries*

3. *Currency*

Now let us look at these 3 points in isolation— looking at the benefits and the bane.

Religion was made to make us all understand the Creator and the creations. Every religion has a mythological bend to it for their followers to understand and live per the governing principles of life. Without religion, the world would have plunged into chaos, and there would have been barbaric, savage rulers and kingdoms that would have done as they pleased—looted, murdered and raped, with no fear of tomorrow, no remorse and no positive feelings towards each other.

We all need to understand and decide for ourselves if religion has, is and will help us get integrated or will it separate us based on the way our belief systems, traditions and cultures evolve? Surely, the Creator wants us all to reside in peace and harmony with each other and Mother Nature. If our religions are doing the same and as per the directions of the Creator, then we are on the right track.

But alas! Religion is also being used to destroy people —the very same people that God created to live in harmony with each other. It is being used to bend the cardinal rules and is being misinterpreted and causing human kind to hate and even kill one another. In this mode, people have created a path of destruction to life and property, giving rise to untold miseries and sufferings.

However, this is not just today and with what is happening around the world. Religion has been used in the past to destroy beautiful works of art, monuments, people, and lives—the very life that created religion. All this without a thought given to the grander and bigger picture and without asking the simple question to our conscience—*Would our Lord want this and be happy with our doings?*

God never made demarcations; He gave us all this land and the resources to live on it. As the human race grew and developed, so did our minds, lust and greed for power. The moment that seed of usurping power and becoming the political or religious leader germinated in the mind, the demise of humans began—the "control" gene in some of us started going into overdrive and started creating problems as the leaders started creating groups and defining boundaries.

For centuries, there have been crusaders, fighters, usurpers, murderers, armies and kings, political leaders and we see there is a person at the top that controls—some do well, and some don't. Today, we have countries and states being united, or breaking up, based on differing opinions of their leaders.

The good part of having kingdoms and countries is that it is better managed if it is small. It keeps the local interest of the citizens in mind, is easier to govern and get things done quickly while arresting corruption and malpractices.

Smaller kingdoms and countries make it easier to have people that bond on a cultural, social, religious and spiritual plane. The disadvantages are that it leads to other problems of infiltration, protectionism, creating defense forces and intelligence agencies, which can then result in fomenting trouble and creating instabilities in the region.

In some cases, a powerful force that others must bend down to, or be wary of creating fear and indignation, is not liked by many. But, a large country also gives economies of scale which can then be enjoyed by its citizens.

We all used to live on a barter system. If I was a farmer and needed clothes, I would give a bag of grains in exchange for a shirt from the weaver, who in turn would get help from the doctor and give something in return and so on and so forth.

This carried on for some time till the kingdoms formed and mankind created another great tool to do trade—money! I feel this has robbed humans of their peace of mind and given rise to miseries for many.

While money is obviously good and is the tool to buy, acquire and do transactions today, the problem is that the concept of money has created unscrupulous ways and wants of hoarding more of it. More money equates to more wealth, which in turn equates to more power.

The ability to get things done is directly proportional today to the amount of money a person has, how rich and powerful they are, and how much they can afford. This gave rise to the capitalist society, which does not care about the poor or downtrodden, who often end up working hard and at times get the wrong end of the deal.

It is every person for themselves, and you start

wondering, did God want this? Would He be proud of what we are doing?

These have given rise to problems, imbalances and deficits in our society, and have given rise to corruption, crime and hatred. Surely there is more to this than what meets the eye. When the Creator can and has created such a wonderful world, surely, He could have created a more perfect world and made everyone be in peace and harmony with each other with no fear, anxiety or depression.

Or, are we saying that God has the power to create everything and has control of everything, except for the way the human brain works and evolves. I find this very illogical and will stay with the belief I have in that He has the power to do much more.

Our human brain is limited and cannot contemplate what He is possible of creating, destroying and doing. So, there must be a reason for the way things are and the way they are happening.

We are told by our gurus, priests, elders and others to forgive and forget. Some religious leaders and zealots ask people to behave in a certain way. Some go to the extent of saying that their religion is most supreme and others should follow the same. In the past, tribes and kingdoms have been decimated and destroyed based on religion.

Places of worship have been destroyed, and the doings of men in the aftermath has been a sacrilege. Most people don't know what they are doing; they go by what their leaders tell them to.

I wish everyone would pause, asked their inner conscience and then went about doing the task they are carrying out as told by their religious or political leaders. If we did a self-check every time we were to harm someone verbally, mentally or physically, the world would be an even better place and we would be even more peaceful with others but most importantly with oneself.

More often than not, the reason behind the way our leaders react and guide the people innocently listening to every word they say is sadly driven by this tool that we have created–money!

So I beg to ask this question again—If all this is going on, why is it going unchecked? There is no bad God or Demon or the Devil, as God created the universe and everything in it. Then why is our most respected, worshiped and loved God allowing all of this to happen? Why is He not doing something to intervene?

Why are there evil forces on the planet–the rich and unscrupulous, which many times seem to be getting their way while the honest citizen is being penalized? Why are there handicapped people and lepers, misery and hunger, people dying and deceiving?

What is truly happening out there?

Millions of times this question has been asked, and the answer has been either, *I don't know, God only knows*, or some of the spiritual masters have tried explaining it in their own way. But surely there must be a connection between what is happening and the grander design for us and our lives?

In a world where everything has answers; where

everything happens for a reason; where everything that has been created has been to support some form of the life systems on the planet, what could be the connection between all that we see, all that we seek and our existence?

What is the meaning of existence?

What is the meaning of life?

Oraciones, 2013

CHAPTER THREE

————◦————

WHO AM I?

Many people who are more spiritually inclined have asked this question: who am I? Along with the question, there have been hundreds of hypotheses on this topic and on existence.

The spiritual masters have defined "I" to be:

1. A spark

2. A quantum of energy

3. A Soul

4. Part of a larger universe

5. Part of God

Whatever we are, the connection between our body and "I" is what most people consider as life. It is that bridge between the material and spiritual life. But most of the doctrines or the answers have not answered the question: Why am I not in control?

A quick understanding of this "I," or the Soul, is needed and where we come from. Rebirth, karma, dharma… what has happened will happen again, whatever happens, is for good, people come to influence your thoughts… sounds familiar? Let me explain.

It has been explained to us that the Soul never dies. Just like energy flows from one form to another, so does the Soul from one body to another. The Soul, just like a spark of energy, can never be created or destroyed but just passes on from one body form to another.

Some of the scriptures and teachings, I feel, offer some deeper explanation of where man came from and where he is going. When we die, the mind, with all the tendencies, preferences, abilities and characteristics that have been developed and conditioned in this life, re-establishes itself in a new being.

Thus, the new individual grows and develops a personality conditioned both by the previous mental characteristics and by the new environment. This journey of life based on experiences from the past and actions of the present then determines what happens next.

The personality of the current body will be modified by conscious effort and conditioning factors like education, parental influence and society, but once again after death, will re-establish itself as a new life in a new being.

The process of dying and being reborn will continue until the conditions that cause it, the mental factors of craving and ignorance, cease. When they do, instead of being reborn, the mind attains a state called Nirvana or of eternal peace and bliss.

When there is no more activity in the brain, no

longing and no desires, it signifies the soul to have reached that level of supreme consciousness which many believe is the ultimate state to be achieved and which is akin to that of the Creator.

How does the Soul go from one body to another? When a person is dying, he loses conscious control of his mental processes. There comes a time when the actions and habits locked away in his memories, are released. In many instances, a mental image arises in his mind. This image is totally involuntarily and is produced by his karma, or past actions.

Depending upon the nature of the karma that produces this image, the person may see dark shadowy figures, frightening images, his relatives or perhaps visions of scenic beauty. Quite often, he will cry out at these visions or remark about them to his visitors. Even though the physical body may be weak, these thought units are very strong as death approaches.

When the body finally breaks down at the point of death, these energies are released as mental energy.

Energy Balancer, 2003

As energy cannot be destroyed, these units must re-establish themselves in a new body thus causing the phenomenon of rebirth.

Think of it being like radio waves that comprise energy at different frequencies, which are then transmitted and picked up by the receiver from where the radio reproduces them as words and music. It is the same with that of the mind.

At death, mental energy travels through space, is picked up by the fertilized egg of the future mother, is reborn as a new being and manifests itself as a new personality. The mind acts as the receiver as well as the broadcast station. So do other people's minds, which are also emitting and receiving vibrations and frequencies of thoughts, actions, persons and location.

The intersecting frequency emitted, and received, is what gives birth to an individual. Thus, it is important that a dying person is comforted and reminded of his good deeds. He should not be made confused and visitors should not overtly grieve in his presence. This is to negate the longing and the attachment and the desire that gets created by the thought of getting close together with the near, dear and grieving individuals.

Neither should unfamiliar ideas be introduced to him. Rather the person should be reminded that the final destination is the Creator and to be with him and to focus on him. Each of our scriptures says that we should chant or remember the name of our Gods while dying to achieve heavenly status with them.

Our scriptures are again common in this belief. We say, "Oh Jesus," "Allah," "Hare Krishna", "Buddham saranam gacchami" and other Gods that we bow to and believe chanting their name will bring us closer to them. When we die, and utter their names, we will be drawn to them and will be like them-liberated from this world.

Hope that is what mankind wants to achieve–total bliss and peace in the heavenly abode as, if you wanted to be rich, famous and especially thought about that while you breathed your last, that would give rise to a desire and the entire cycle of fulfillment would start.

Instead, not having the desire would get you a step closer to being fully liberated and close to the Creator. You may ask is that not a desire in itself. Yes it is and this is the only desire that is not going to get you back into the circle of life but will free you from it. The spiritual desire is the only one that is exempt and is allowed in this test called life.

Another question that comes up time and again-Is one always reborn as a human being?

No, there are several realms into which one can be reborn. Some people are reborn in heavenly planes, some are reborn as human beings or animals or a different species. Heaven is not a place; it is a state of existence where one has a subtle body and where the mind experiences mostly pleasure.

Some believe and strive very hard to be reborn in a heavenly existence, believing it to be a permanent state. But it is not. Like all conditioned states, heaven is impermanent and when one's life span is finished there, one could well be reborn again as a human.

I feel there is a desire even out there in the heavens. After a very long time, the soul would like to possibly get an experience of a certain species, situation or place or it could be that it would be prayed to and summoned by a living species or in some cases, the rested and realized soul would like to go out and help a needy person or animal.

If that happens, there are two ways this could go— the soul comes down to the planet for a brief period in time and fulfills that wish, desire, help and goes back to where it came from and it's heavenly abode.

The other thing that could happen is if the soul unknowingly and unwittingly gets involved with another place, person or thing and a desire creeps in, the entire cycle of desire, fulfillment and life starts all over.

Think of it as a person being summoned by prayers. You, of course cannot summon a person or the soul and have that happen in a jiffy. A lot of penance, extreme meditation and pure thoughts over an extended period of time (can be even years) is needed and it also depends on the soul of the person being summoned.

While the Creator's energy spark manifests itself as that being to help out, it is possible that this life form gets attached to a child, lady or man or even a community or place. If that energy spark or Soul is realized enough, it can finish it's duty for the reason it took the human form and go back to the heavens but if it gets engrossed and interested, it would break the cardinal rules and start behaving like any normal human being.

That peaked interest would give rise to a desire which is not spiritual but some thing else and that would in turn give rise to another life cycle, another story and the cycle of life and death and liberty would continue.

Hell, likewise, is not a place but a state of existence where one has a subtle body and where the mind experiences mainly anxiety and distress. Being a ghost, again, is a state of existence where the body is subtle and where the mind is continually plagued by longing and dissatisfaction.

Heavenly beings experience mainly pleasure, hell beings and ghosts experience mainly pain and human beings experience usually a mixture of both. So, the main difference between the human realm and other realms is the body and mind type and the quality of experience.

There is another point to note here as well. It's not that there are 3 separate planes (Heaven, Hell and Earth), all these exist at any given time in the same place. One person can realize utmost bliss on Earth and feel that this is heaven.

The same person can be driven to the corner by circumstances and some even take their lives thinking to live is to be in Hell and others just don't see it that way. It seems the definitions of these 3 states depend on our experiences in Life and maybe our past lives as well. Could it be that a person does not go to heaven, but rather has a good life?

Here's another point to think of: say a person of religion "A" kills another person of religion "B" just based on not being of the same religion and beliefs. It has obviously not occurred to them that after death, they can be born to the same religion "B." It has also obviously not crossed their mind that they are killing their brother or sister, if one believes that God created everyone as equal.

The bad acts we do are all so situational, with no connection to our inner self, or consciousness. It is mindless and we should ask ourselves before we harm another, "What good does it do?" or "What does it achieve?"

To those who are killing or hating each other today based on religious beliefs and sentiments, I would request them to get a DNA test done. No one wants to trace back their DNA and their genes to find that maybe their great-great-great-great-great grandfather was in fact the same or we are from the same family tree!

I feel that the more you think about a person, situation or context, you are sending out waves in the universe and you will get paired to the thing that you love or detest the most.

What I am trying to get to here is that it's important to think before you kill or harm a person. You never know, you may just join them or have a time when the roles and positions will get switched and you will be at the receiving end. So, what is the point?

This doesn't just apply to killing based on religion, country or society. This pertains to our daily lives, at school, at work and at play. I am sure many of us have faced a situation where we have witnessed someone stepping on someone or putting down someone to get a role, promotion or raise or recognition.

Whenever we try doing something like this, we need to listen to our inner conscience, which will rein us back from doing anything wrong. But, do we care? Who has the time? Life is short, so get on with it!

Sadly, some of us have this attitude but each of these has far reaching implications and meanings, more than we can imagine. That is why it is good to read this and the scriptures, knowing that this life is not the end. We cannot just afford to do anything we want thinking "What the heck," "Who cares" and "Who will know?" And even if we do, we should mindfully and consciously try and be good and do good to others.

We are being watched, every action and deed is being recorded and will stand testament when the time comes. Which brings me to the next topic of birth; what decides where we will be born or reborn?

This is where I want to introduce in more detail the theory of karma. I have referenced karma a few times before and folks around the world always use it, but what is it? Is it a person, place, situation or thing?

Simply put, karma is our actions. If we are good and take positive steps, we have good karma. On the other hand, if we think or do evil, we collect and have bad karma. Think of it as a Soul currency. We earn credits with good karma and have a good credit rating.

On the other hand, score low and you will have

bad or negative credit with bad karma. God is like our Universal CFO (Chief Financial Officer). If we have bad karma, we owe more good karma back to the Universal lender or God and with interest. If we have good karma and keep building on it, we will get good interest on the good karma and get better lives, situations, relations and opportunities.

Karma has a very big role to play in our lives. We are continuously under scrutiny and our sub-consciousness is like a flight recorder's black box that keeps recording our karma as we continue our daily lives. Think or do good and you will earn credits, or good karma. If you think or do bad, you'll earn discredit, or bad karma. At the end of our lives, once we reach Judgment Day, our karma determines where we go next in our spiritual lives.

Why is it important to have good karma? Reason being, if you only have good karma, then you have a chance to advance in your spiritual journey. Your Soul will be able to advance and demand a higher plane or celestial context to reach and attain.

The stronger your good karma is, the more realized

you will be, or at least get a chance to become, more realized. What does becoming more realized mean? It means the distinction between our three states of sub-consciousness, consciousness and super-consciousness, will diminish and we will see everything as one.

This is again like the 3 planes that we can relate to. The sub-consciousness or the conscience is what is deep within us—this is what guides us and has that gut feeling or the 6th sense and has a chord to our super-soul and the Creator. The consciousness is the present and what our brains and sensory organs feel and see—it's our material world. The super-consciousness is the realized and liberated world of the Creator or the heavenly abode.

The trick is to connect our subconscious self to the super-conscious self and remove the middle part which is our current conscious or worldly state. The middle or conscious or our current material world is the only part where we have a name, an individuality, thereby the concept of "I" and with it - ego. We need to eradicate this ego, this "I" within us and understand and be part of this grand universe understanding that we came from there and we will go back there. This life is just a stage where we or "I" am playing my part. This is the wall that needs to be broken down to connect with the Creator. That's why I say it's a pretty small and simple step but very hard and complex to understand and do.

We will then get closer and closer to our heavenly abode. The whole universe and everything in it will start to make more sense. Till then, everything will be either rubbish, unknown or something attributed to the supernatural. Only the realized Soul can make sense of it all. The only path to becoming a realized Soul is to build good karma.

If you have bad karma, you will either go to Hell or be in a situation full of anxiety, depression, restlessness, hatred, fear, internal commotion and turmoil, as well as full of adversaries and difficult situations. One should realize that this did not happen by chance, but has been the result of the person's karma.

Depending on the amount of bad karma, one may have to repent for their sins and get a chance to improve their Karmic score for not only that birth, but many more births and lives to come. If you do further evil, you are going to end up in a spiral fall into a deep well of Hell from where it will be difficult to come out of.

The only way out is to be good and righteous. If you do good and continue doing good, you will find that you will be enjoying a better life, one full of bliss, happiness, wealth, friends, opportunities and supporters. The better you are, the better you will beget. *You reap what you sow*. That is why one might say, *I pray, lead a good life, treat everyone with dignity and respect, don't harm anyone or animals and still, why did I deserve this?* It's your past life's karma that is working itself out on you and your current life.

Just keep doing what you were by being good and sure enough, your life will turn for the better in this or in a different life. That is why this is a game and it is so interesting—it does not end with one stroke. It goes on and on.

As long, as there is life, you are bound to have

all kinds of folks around you—some unfortunate, some the same as you and some very fortunate. But even amongst them all, you will have the good, the bad and the ugly.

And all I can say is that this life is not the end. Yes, it is true that we have come here in our lives based on the past deeds, based on our past desires and wishes, and based on the call of the other connected Souls. You might say if everything is predetermined and defined, what can we really change? I believe the answer to that is—We have some quota or some part of our lives or decisions that we make that is left to ourselves.

These decisions and actions that we choose to take can change ours and the others' futures—this again depends also on our karma, which is based on our thoughts, words and actions—it's cyclical and hence we call it the circle of life.

One's karma will determine where the person goes next, what kind he or she will be born as—with abnormalities or with a healthy body and mind; on the street or in the palace; with or without loved ones around—and a host of other factors. We are born again and again till we collect enough of good karma and become realized and become one with God.

There have been many experiments conducted to prove the concept of the Soul and its existence and of the Soul-taking rebirth. How else would one explain so many cases where the person recounts people, memories and situations from their past birth? One such example is of a three-year-old boy who lived on the border of Israel and Giza.

He remembered details on how he was killed, where he was buried and what was the weapon used. When researchers took up this case, the boy guided them to the exact site where his past life's body and the murder weapon used were buried.

There have been many scientists who have experimented to find out what happens to the Soul when it leaves a body. Here is an example that has tried to prove that the Soul exists and would leave the human body upon death.

In the nineties, Dr. Konstantin Korotkov, a Director in St. Petersburg, Russia tried a unique way of photographing the Soul using Kirlian photography. Dr. Korotkov used this technique using gas discharge visualization (GDV). According to some of the Chinese and Hindu scriptures, our body has 7 electric meridian points called chakras.

Imagine a person sitting in a squatting position and a vertical line running from the head to the base of the spine, dividing the body into 2 equal halves. The chakras start above the head, mind, throat, chest, solar plexus, lower abdomen and the base of our spine.

Dr. Korotkov used this principle and associated different colors to each of the chakras, and using a CCD (charge coupled device) camera, transposed to a computer, could photograph the aura of the body with colors.

This made it easier to see the movements of our body and Soul, very much like what happens during an angiography—they inject colored dye to study the blood flow in different organs and vessels in our body.

In one such study done on a dying person, Dr. Korotkov showed that there was something that moved out of the body at death and up into the atmosphere thus suggesting that there was indeed something like a Soul, or energy form that moved out of our bodies at death.

This proves that the Soul or energy was trapped in the human body, but moved upwards and out of the body post death. Per Dr. Korotkov, the head and the navel are the first to lose the life and the final parts of a body to lose consciousness are the heart and the groin. This has also been proved by experiments that we have done in our laboratories in school.

When you dissect a frog, though the frog is technically dead, it sometimes continues to have a heart that keeps on beating for a while till the whole body becomes still and motionless.

If you see some of the pictures or videos of Dr. Korotkov's experiments, you will see something like a life form moving out from the body and going up and vanishing—this life form is what he and we call the Soul.

Similarly, another experiment was keeping a dying body in a thick air-tight glass container and post death, a hole was found on the thick glass top suggesting that something had moved out of that body at the time of its death—an energy form—the Soul. There are different debates on this experiment: some do not believe the Soul exists, others say that the Soul cannot be felt and would not be able to break a physical object, like glass.

There are some that believe that this could indeed be possible if the Soul is to be thought of as a spark of energy. The late Professor Ian Stevenson from Virginia University's department of Psychology studied students and children for many years.

He published anecdotal evidences that the mind of the subjects was astonishingly aware of things they could not otherwise have been, unless it was programmed into their minds at birth or that these were subjects of rebirth! Following his footsteps, was another psychiatry professor at the University of Virginia—Jim Tucker.

Tucker too compiled many cases that point to the theory of the Soul and rebirth of the Soul. One such example is that of a 4-year-old boy called Ryan in Oklahoma, United States.

Though so little, he used to direct imaginary movies but at night he would get nightmares and start screaming. His parents took him to the doctor who said that it was normal for kids to have nightmares and he would outgrow them as he aged. His parents were at ease till one night Ryan told his mom, "Mama, I think I used to be someone else. I remember a big house with a pool in Hollywood.*"*

That is when his parents started getting serious on what he was saying and started researching more on Hollywood, movies, theaters, events, places and people. One day, they were going through a book that had a still photograph of the 1930's movie *Night after Night*.

There were two men surrounded by four others and Ryan pointed his little finger at one of the men and said— "That's me. I used to be that man. And that is George, I worked with him in this film." Ryan's parents were astonished on seeing and hearing this and after doing lots of research, they found out that man he was pointing to was George Raft and their son Ryan, was a little-known actor of those times, *Marty Martin*!

There is another example of a two-year-old boy in Louisiana, James Leininger, who loved toy planes but frequently used to slam the toy planes onto the table, so hard that it came across as odd. James used to scream, "Airplane crash on fire." Also, that he had been a pilot and flown off a boat.

On being asked which plane or boat James said, "*Natoma*." His father thought it sounded Japanese, but James said that it was American. Based on this information, his father, after a lot of research, found that there indeed used to be an American aircraft carrier named the *USS Natoma Bay*.

During one of the operations during World War II, there was one person lost due to one of the planes crashing into the sea and sinking, giving a whole lot of credibility to James' story. James turned out to be the pilot whose plane had nosedived into the water and was killed in the accident.

There are many such scientists who have conducted experiments that show not everything follows a hereditary pattern and evolution is not the answer to everything. It is one aspect, but there are so many more that we are trying to see in this manuscript.

So, for a moment, let us accept that the Soul exists and give in to the fact that the Soul can travel, enter another body and is what kindles and starts a life. But, what is it? What is the Soul made up of? How was it created and how does it get destroyed? Why do I have to understand more about it and more importantly, what is in it for me?

The Soul, the spark or the energy manifestation goes on from one body to the next, depending on the frequency and the thoughts that seek it. It also moves from one body to another or one situation to another depending on the past words and actions.

There is a saying, *Ask the universe what you want*

Orancion, 2013

and the universe will start working towards your wish. Of course, your resolve should be strong and sustained. One cannot say, *I want to be rich on day one, be married to the royal family on day two and to win the country's elections on day three.*

It must be the same yearning day after day, week after week, month after month, year after year and most times and depending on your karma, you will start getting it either in that birth, or in a subsequent birth. But, remember you as the body will not get it and you as the eternal Soul, will. It's almost like there are two people and forces in us—one that is the body and mind, while the other is the Soul.

You will hear people tell you to go by your gut feeling. It is not your gut, but your inner or sub-consciousness that they are making a reference to. This is important! It seems like there is a dual force that determines your tomorrow—your past actions, karma and your desires. Having desires is another way to create tomorrow. If you really and truly yearn and desire for something, the universe will work and give it to you.

Provided you meet the qualification criteria and that will create another situation, place, a fresh group of people and characters and with it will come the benefits, problems and challenges. So, the more we yearn and desire, the more we create and the cycle of life and creation moves on.

The ideal state and what we call "Godly" is to:

1. Have zero desires

2. Have zero in our Karmic account–great to have positive but at least a zero!

3. Have no reaction

4. Just flow

This is a state where there are no desires and cravings. There is nothing left for us to achieve or atone for. The mind is completely at rest. There is no ego and we are like a giant rock on the beach—calm and undeterred by the waves of turmoil, despair and challenges that hits us. This is a state where there is zero activity in our brains and we don't respond to what is going on outside.

The mind is at complete bliss and rest. Whether there is someone shouting, abusing, whether there are good or bad things happening around the person, the person sees all of the happenings in the same light and as different frequencies of our same loving universe.

There is an ability to see through and far into the different people, situations and actions—that this is all connected and a part of the same force. It is like being in a state of penultimate meditation–a state called Nirvana!

I guess by now, you know that there is no you, or I, we are just manifestations of our thoughts which are brought to life by a Soul. The thoughts and desires give rise to the platform, setting or the environment in which we are born. For example, a beggar on the street or a king in a palace. We are just the amalgamation of Thought-Body-Karma-Soul put together.

We know that *energy can neither be created nor*

destroyed but changes it's form from one to another as quoted by Einstein. In the same vein, the Soul also changes its form from one to another. It can be light at one time, a human in another, a tree another time and a cloud in another.

The Soul or energy form is all part of the same Grand Creation and simply moves from one physical form to the other pretty much like a butterfly moves from one flower to the next. You can call this movement a game, a cosmic rhythm or God's will but that is the nature and the meaning of our existence.

We create, give birth, destroy, die and give rise to more stories, lives and civilizations. This cumulative, or exponential, cosmic dance continues, reaches a height, dissolves and self-destructs into nothingness. After a while (a few billion years), this entire cycle of creation and destruction starts all over again.

Profess whatever faith or religion you want, simply remember that there is a Judgment day! It does not matter whether you believe in the Soul, karma or some of the other points, but what does matter is that you will be much better off spreading love, peace and harmony than by spreading hatred, disharmony and crime. There should not be any differing opinions on that.

This is the teaching and understanding in most of our religious scriptures as well. That is why our holy scriptures tells us to think no evil and do no bad. Also, to be good and righteous, while being good to yourself and to others.

That is the only way you can go for a better life in the next birth and onwards. It's like amassing a positive currency in your bank account. This currency is of our deeds—good and bad. The more good deeds you have to your credit, the more realized you are and the more qualified you are to go to God, or the Heavens.

The more you owe or have bad deeds to your credit, the more you must repent and pay for. Many of us don't consider the ramifications of our actions or words. You do not have to take lives, murder someone or rob a bank to score a bad deed.

Pilgrim, Soul Liberty 2011

Anything bad you think, say or do could set the score. You may lie, cheat, say something to hurt another person, better your own interests, ridicule or criticize someone—remember all of these go towards your negative credit account.

Normally, people should ask themselves, *Is this for real?* And then they should go about their lives but alas, we have the majority of our population who say, *Who knows if all this is true, we have our own lives—let's move on with it! I have no time for all this. I have a job and family to take care of.* All I am trying to stress here is that while we go on, even if we don't care, we should make it a priority and try not to think, say or do bad to any person, place or thing. After all, that is what our scriptures say, right?

But, I think it is worth taking a short pause and going over this. I would ask what have we got to lose if we try to be good in words and action? Sometimes things said to your loved ones, people at work or in society are involuntary, but that is when the consciousness evolves and guides the person doing or saying anything wrong.

A person who takes another's life, cheats or robs someone surely has a dead conscience—we know that. On the other hand, a person who is pious, gives to others and is selfless gains more in their spiritual standing and awareness.

The universe manifests itself to give you a chance; you are created or given birth to pay off your debt and get into a credit of good deeds. You may not be able to have an immediate control over your destiny but in the long run you will, provided you let your conscience guide you.

Remember your life is not just this life that you see but a long life from the creation of your soul from the Creator to the entire journey till it comes back and merges with the Creator. This life is like one of the chapters of your cosmic journey.

The only way you can change your otherwise set destiny is the power of your thoughts and actions in your current life and how you conduct yourself especially when life throws a choice or a situation in front of you where you must decide. That decision depending on how many other lives is it affecting will have more profound effects and ramifications than you can imagine.

But fret not—do what you think is right given your understanding at that moment and you should be fine. Just do not harm anyone for whatever reason.

I know at times that this can be perplex and difficult. You can be in the corporate world, a business or profession that sometimes might make you say or do something you did not intend to. But, if there is a reason for not doing something lest it should harm or cheat someone, one should desist from doing it.

Sometimes you cannot help it. Remember everything is so intertwined that sometimes it's simply meant to be. We walk and drive on the roads and never think of the millions of small insects and lives that we kill.

There is a sect of Jainism in India and in Buddhists who go to the extent of covering their mouths to not allow insects or bacteria to get in and get killed–true it's a little extreme, but look at the thought behind the action—it's so very positive!

But does that mean we are doomed–of course not! You cannot have a mosquito or a snake on your body and think, *what a bad thing it would be to kill it*–you have to do what you have to do, but it's the thought that counts. If you are killing an animal to save your, or someone's life, it's a good thing and considered as a credit.

But, if you are killing for recreation, an act of vengeance or simply harming when there was no need to, that's too bad—its' going to go against you either way. Somewhere down the line as you take subsequent rebirths, there will come a time where you will go through the same situation where you will be born as that same type of animal you harmed or killed or be born to experience that same adverse and opposing situation of pain and suffering.

This is done just to make you realize the folly that you had done. It's not payback time, but a way to show the person the other side of the story and make them and their souls or inner consciousness aware of the harmed person or animal and what their family goes through.

True—we commit a lot of harm to other people, animals and other beings without understanding the deeper meaning our actions have on them and their families. But, once this thought starts being a seed in our minds, we will be more mindful as we conduct our lives and as we interact with one another.

You might be wondering as to why our memory is flushed when we are born. I believe that this is so that we do not have preconceived notions, doctrines or dogmas. These would otherwise cloud our minds and prevent us from leading a normal life, which gives us a chance to be our own self, free from the past and freewheeling in the present.

Therefore, it is good to be cognizant about all of this and go about conducting our lives. The other option is always there—*heck with all this, who cares?*

Instead of fighting over religion, faith and countries, we should be trying to spend time helping each other; loving and making things and life better for one another. Love, compassion, kindness and understanding will get us much more in the long run than anything else.

We have seen that our actions, also called karma, is the collection of currency in our bank account that defines our lives and the way to increase our bank account deposit is to have good karma and which can only be achieved through good and pure thoughts and actions.

CHAPTER FOUR

MODERN DAY REFERENCES

Our songs, culture, places of worship and movies have started depicting the theories of life and life-after-death. They also theorize how we were born and could exist in different ways. Once we delve deeper into their meanings, it starts making more sense and ignites that thought in ourselves on what the grand design is all about and answering the question, *What are we doing?*

Should we not be better off doing something good and meaningful, instead of trying to hurt or kill someone else? Why should we strive to be a better

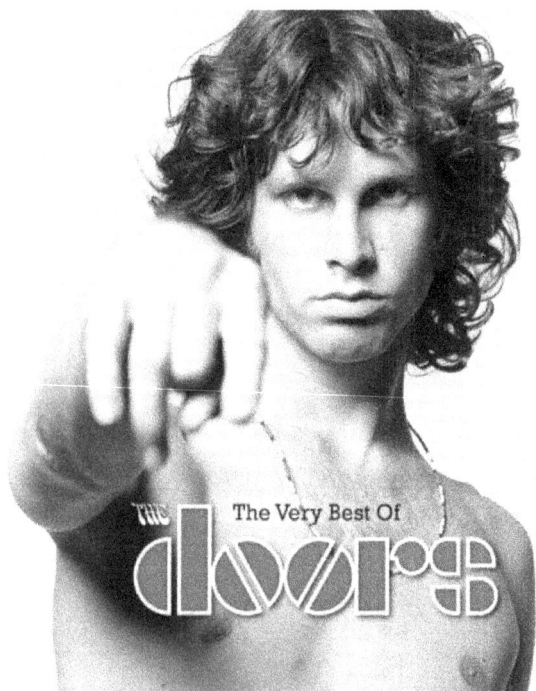

The Doors, 2007

person and how it can affect our lives—from now to the many and future births?

Jim Morrison and his band used to play in Los Angeles in a club called Whiskey Go-Go. While he was from a reasonably well-heeled family, there were problems between his parents. Jim used to write his lyrics mostly when he was tripping on acid, and he sought refuge in drugs at a very young age. He used to think of harming his father and had different views of life and the end.

To him, the end meant many things, as it was evident from his songs and lyrics. He wanted to end the miseries of his mother, put an end to his father and bring about an end to his suffering and an end to his life.

He was twenty-eight-years-old when he passed away. He is said to have penned in these last lyrics to the beautiful and meaningful, yet controversial songs he used to sing and has left for us and the future generations to come.

This is the end, beautiful friend

This is the end, my only friend, the end
Of our elaborate plans, the end
Of everything that stands, the end
No safety or surprise, the end
I'll never look into your eyes, again
Can you picture what will be, so limitless and free
Desperately in need, of some, stranger's hand
In a, desperate land...

Jim "Mojo" Morrison was reputed for many of his off-screen and on-screen antics, but his lyrics beg a better and deeper meaning. Why would a person who used to do drugs go to lengths to write about the end being beautiful? Who is the stranger? What or where is that desperate land? Does it all seem simple, or very cosmic?

Here is another one of his epic songs–"The Other Side."

You know the day destroys the night
Night divides the day
Tried to run
Tried to hide
Break on through to the other side

Break on through to the other side
Break on through to the other side, yeah
We chased our pleasures here
Dug our treasures there
But can you still recall
The time we cried
Break on through to the other side
Break on through to the other side
Yeah!

Legend has it that Jim used to be heavily into sex and drugs. What he meant by this song is that we have had enough of the material world and it was time to break on through to the other, more real and meaningful side of life—far from the pangs of the unreal and dreamy like scenario created by a world of sex and drugs.

We know the problem is both have highs, which are short-lived and not sustainable. So he was asking for another world that would have more lasting love, peace and comfort.

Agreed, his lyrics are still not fully understood, and many folks dismiss his works and his antics as that of a junkie, but I think there was more to the man. How on Earth would a young guy like him, steeped in problems, have drugs and still be able to speak such deep and insightful things about life and life-after-death?

Jim is saying that we have made our fortunes or have done something evil, and we still try to run and cry. But, there is the yearning to go to the *other side* where there will not be any misery, pain or evil, but there will be a place very serene and surreal— the Heavens!

Let's take another more recent example where movies try to break it down and give a new meaning to technological, biological, genetic, mechanical, cosmic evolution and revolution. I am speaking about the movie–*The Matrix*! I was very captivated by what it embodied and tried to depict, and have watched it and its sequels many times.

Each time I see the movie, it brings in a slightly different understanding of who we are. We are all programs (lives as we know ourselves today) that have a beginning and an end. For example, our genetic codes are programmed within us, which makes us the way we are and defines how we behave. But, let's visit this more in depth later on in the book.

The Matrix and some of its sequels depict that there are two worlds—a physical and a metaphysical world. While the physical world is the one where we all should be in and is the real or realized world, there is a makeshift world or cyber world namely Earth.

The inhabitants are all programs, and each program or life form has a definitive beginning and end. Neo, played by Keanu Reeves, and the team are trying to break the sullenness and direction-less earthlings to find and show them a way to break out of this false shell they are living in, this false world on Earth.

In the process, Neo and the others fight the evil forces who are trying to control and let the human beings work the way they are accustomed to and not let mankind see beyond what they see. Neo, on the other hand, is trying to show that everything has a purpose, and while we have a beginning and an end, we also have an exit path that is not death.

One that can take us out of this fictitious world we live in and get out to the real world. I think it is very interesting and the topic is so deep and thought provoking. It can make you feel that the movie is rubbish and it is just our imagination, or for people like me, it plays into the very essence of what I and many others think about as to the meaning of it all and what is going on out there.

Sure Presidents, companies, jobs and relationships come and go, but is this all a life that we are sometimes haplessly destined for, or is this just a speck of the grand design?

There are points in *The Matrix* that made me feel that I should reference it; as many of the thoughts or ideas, that I am putting in this book, resemble what has been depicted in the movie.

Take for example the fact that Neo is asked to take a blue or red pill. Or, many other parts of the movie where one has to make that choice. You never know what is on the other side of the door till you choose

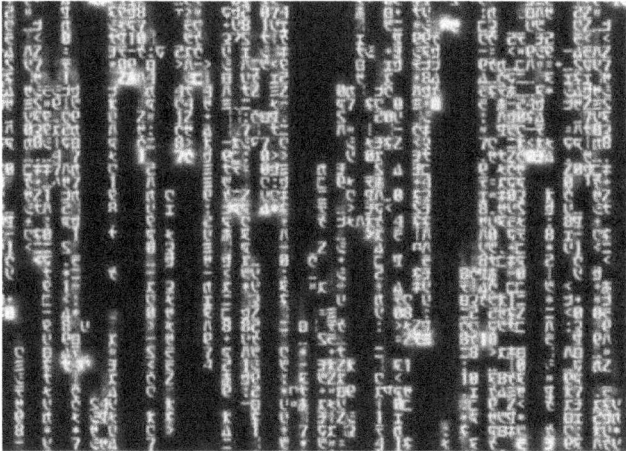

Google, Wallpaper, 2009

and enter through that door. But that is what makes life so exciting. We may not realize we are facing choices every day, and the door that opens based on our choice leads to an altogether different road ahead which brings with it more surprises, challenges, opportunities and problems. This is akin to what we saw earlier as well—whenever we come across a challenge or a problem, a door or two appear in front of us and our journey is dependent on the choice we make. This is where we wield the power and own our destiny while the rest of it is pretty much cast out.

Depending on the door that we open and the choice we make, opportunities can arise for us, and we can make the best of them, or we can make a bad choice that would make us omit those opportunities altogether. Again, this is not that we missed the boat.

There will be another opportunity or door that will present itself based on our karma and our desires, but we will have to wait it out till that time is right again. Hence, we hear the phrases *Seize the opportunity* or *Seize the moment*.

We don't even get to understand this as we are in a worldly life full of trains, cars, job schedules, schools, friends, relatives and then there are only so many hours during the day, and our body needs to rest. Almost a third or fourth of our time is spent sleeping and resting.

It is for this reason that many of the spiritual masters choose to go to the forests, hills, or caves to be away from all the hustle and bustle of the cities. They would move close to nature and hear the cosmic sounds and the vibrations, for the one who catches these does not need anything else.

But again, everyone who reads this book, or does not have time to, will not go into the forest or meditate and try to listen or understand the deeper meaning to our lives. There are our families, our jobs, our goals and primary interests, which we need to pursue—isn't there? Yes, but we can spread love and happiness at home, places of work and worship, in fact everywhere.

I see many people mocking spirituality and not trying to understand or acknowledge the deeper meanings of the universe and even going to the extent of saying that it is a waste of time. I could be wrong, but I also see a lot of people asking the same questions that I am asking and seeking answers to. There is a lot of craving to understand the bigger picture of life and the meaning of it all especially nowadays.

The good thing is that the thirst for this cosmic understanding and knowledge is growing, both in the spiritual as well as the scientific world.

While some folks are trying to understand the meaning through deep meditation and understanding the scriptures, there are others who are trying to put probes into outer space, listening to the universe and running projects like landing the rover *Curiosity* on planet Mars. As well as trying to understand more about life and how we came into being and what happened.

I believe that the time will come for every one of us in one of our subsequent births when we are ready. Ready to receive these cosmic vibrations, ready to understand what they mean and ready to move to the next level in our lives. Each one of us is a unique and beautiful Soul, and individual with a collection of lots of experiences carried over from the past, which will carry over from the present.

There have been many examples of our physical world and the nether world, which further extends and gives meaning to life, birth, rebirth, death, the Soul and the thought, and all of it is working under the governing rules of the universe. Hopefully, we understand this more. But to take ourselves into the higher planes of ability, we need to know what we can do.

Surely, we can try inventing machines, robots and artificial intelligence, but what we can program robots or machines to do, depends on how much we think they can do and to the extent we think of programming them. But, who programs us?

Who ensures that we as a race and as individuals evolve as well? How do we make sure that our progeny and successive generations are better and stronger and more equipped to handle the future than us?

From here, I want to take you into the journey of evolution, what God Almighty has created to ensure that we don't stagnate as a species. It's a gradual process of moving us forward and onward, a process by which we keep getting better and more equipped to take on the challenges of tomorrow.

A few tens of thousands of years ago, the Earth was our world, and nothing else existed—we were there, and life to us meant life on Earth; we could not think beyond. This was the time of the caveman and primitive tribes who could not think beyond food, sleep, fights and satisfying their carnal desires.

Since then, we progressed and started understanding the laws of nature, the constellations and science in general. The years around a few thousand years B.C. was when the thought started seeping in about the earthly abode and other abodes, be it heaven or hell.

Today, we know even more and are in search of probable life beyond Earth. We now know about planets, solar systems, galaxies and the universe.

There is now more understanding of the Earth that we live on today and that the Earth may, or may not, be inhabitable in a few thousand years—we will explore that as well as we go forward in this discovery process. Going by the past and the amount we have grown and learned as a species in the last 20,000 years, I wonder how much our understanding will change in the next 20,000 years.

This is where evolution is going to play a key role in moving us forward—natures own way of advancing us as a species. Isn't it lovely that someone has already planned all of this for us? But, where are we headed?

There are many other examples where people in the past, and present, have started heeding and paying attention to what is out there. There is a renewed interest in spirituality, not just in the western world, but also in the rest of the world.

The belief that there is something more to life and that the best way to know more is to do better. Spreading happiness and joy is growing by the day. I think with every passing generation, the human race is becoming more loving and encompassing than the generation before it.

Let's read on and explore more.

CHAPTER FIVE

———————◦○◦———————

THEORY OF EVOLUTION

Human Evolution has many theories around it. One is that humans were just put on Earth along with different animals, trees, plants and an ecosystem to help us all live together. I have a fundamental problem with this theory: If that was the case, then how would we move to the next level?

For example, why have our teeth gotten smaller throughout generations—we know that the earlier cavemen had larger teeth as they had to chew and to tear out things.

Similarly, the brain had not evolved fully at that point in time. As humans developed, and so did our brains, we made tools and weapons to hunt animals, which decreased the reliance and need for big and strong teeth. Slowly emerged a species that could outsmart the rest of the species based not on brawn but brain—born was the human race!

Ever wondered why people in different parts of the world look different? Is it a coincidence that people living near the equator are darker skinned and eat rice and curry based diets, which is easier to digest in the heat? Or, why people in the northern regions or the mountains have more of meat and bread, as they need that to keep their body warm?

Why is it that people who've lived in the mountains for generations where there are snowstorms or in desert areas have eyes, noses and their nostrils shaped in a way, which has adapted to nature and to keep away the sand or the cold from getting into the human body?

What I'm trying to get to is that all these different looking folks could not have been put on Earth at different times. What would be the point? I'd rather think they all evolved over the years—millions of years to reach the current state we see everyone in. Each one has adapted to their surroundings and which is another beautiful and thing of wonder— the way the human body adapts and evolves!

It's theorized that first there was water and favorable conditions on Earth, after which life started evolving—we have a lot of agreement from the scientific community. Whether a life form like bacteria formed automatically, was it put onto the Earth by design or was it an accident is debatable.

Some say that life was transported through a comet or asteroid. Others say that we were all created at one instance, but we are all still trying to find exactly what happened and how exactly did life forms originate on Earth.

But, what is theorized and widely accepted, is that we all came from the apes. The bacteria evolved into fish in water, which evolved into amphibians, then into animals including apes, and finally, human kind the way we know it today, came into existence. The art of walking on two legs, the backbone and spinal cord becoming straight and vertical, instead of horizontal like you have in dogs, cats or horses were a part of evolution.

Not just physically, but we evolved mentally as well. We grew the ability to use the brain for more complex tasks—from building a bow and arrow in the medieval times, to the invention of the wheel and finally to the space shuttles of today. We see evolution taking place in leaps and bounds in all spheres of our lives.

The ability to express ourselves has also changed— our art forms, cultures, languages and dialects and diversity in thoughts, all changed in just the past few thousands of years.

Our Earth has been evolving as well. First, a barren planet, then a planet with water, after that a planet with different species and beings, who knows how much more it will evolve. Perhaps, it will cease to exist, maybe to get created again as the same, or a different form.

The land on our beloved planet was once filled with one large piece of land. Over the years, with the

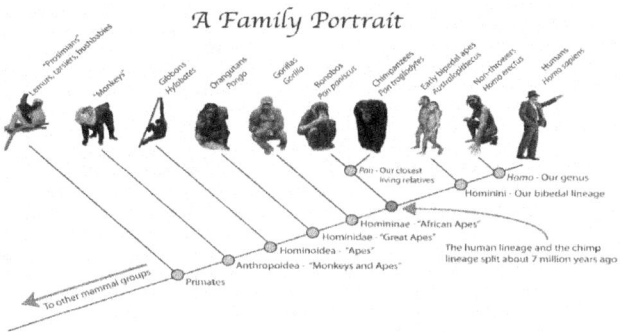

A Family Portrait

Smithsonian Institute, 2016

rotational and gravitational forces, the great tectonic plates shifted, the land masses separated and started drifting further away giving rise to the continents with the oceans coming in between.

There is a lot of evidence that proves this, and it is probably true. We know the coast of Brazil, for example, can fit into the west coast of Africa, and like a jigsaw puzzle, many of the different continents and countries can be brought together to form a single land mass.

If you look at the table on the last page, it shows the way we have evolved over the years. Essentially, what this means is that while we have evolved over the past millions of years, we will continue to evolve over many more millions of years. And then there will be another genetic mutation and split!

Just like we saw the human race being formed, we will find that another species of life being formed better and mightier than the human race, more intelligent and with much higher levels of mental and computing capabilities. Yes, what you are probably thinking is right—we will be the apes of tomorrow!

We will probably find that there will be a new breed of highly evolved human beings who will be far more powerful, physically and mentally, from the ones we know today. You can see this happening already.

Our kids and grandkids are way smarter than we were and the adaptability curve on technology and devices is much higher for them than us, or our previous generations. If this is the case, then in just two to three thousand generations, we can expect to see a higher and more powerful workforce to come into existence.

Earth (if it still exists) or whatever is the system that we will inherit over the next hundreds of thousands of years will be ruled not by humans as we know ourselves today, but by a more evolved species far beyond our comprehension. We will remain, but this advanced species that will get created will rule the Earth and the solar systems and our galaxy.

This evolution and genetic mutations giving rise to

a more advanced life form will keep happening till the advanced species becomes almost like God. As the genetic splits take place, life on Earth will keep advancing and we will get pushed further down the evolution chain. We will be the apes of tomorrow, be the fishes in the Eon after and the ameba of the times after that. And I don't mean we will become apes or that apes will disappear.

As the human species evolve, or rather the new species evolves, we will be pushed further and further down the evolution chain. The other end of the evolution chain will continue growing, and it has one way to go, which is up, and that is towards Godliness.

Whether we get there, or not, or if something happens along the way that stops or aids it, I guess none of us can predict. But, this seems logical in my mind—if I look back at how we have all come about and evolved, it is not too hard to imagine what will happen next.

Sure, the theory of evolution is after all a theory, but in the absence of the truth and when the knowledge does not exist, theories are bound to be there and many of them are not a figment of the imagination. Some of them make sense, some are proven and others—you have to give it time... Well, a lot of time!

Our planet Earth, solar system, galaxy and the universe too will change—we all know that all the celestial bodies also go through a period of evolution. It's not just humans, plants or animal life that is created, lives and then dies. Planets, galaxies and universes do too.

We know about black holes. A black hole is created when the energy of a star reaches a tipping point, and it then collapses upon itself. What happens next is supposed to be a very destructive yet beautiful phenomenon. The black hole collapses into a small area, or circle, but with the same mass as its original size.

This also makes its gravitational force very high, so high that not even light can pass through it. Since light cannot pass through it, it cannot be seen, hence the term "Black Hole."

There are again different theories on how the black holes keep absorbing matter till they reach a threshold. After which instead of collapsing inwards, they explode outwards, and that is the beginning of a new creation of stars, planets, asteroids, comets and the beginning of new life forms.

Modern science believes that quasars contain massive black holes and they, in turn, may represent a stage in the evolution of some galaxies. Let us not get too deep into another interesting topic of how the universe was created. Again, lots of theories and books have been written on the topic.

Mankind is just searching for answers, which it knows nothing about. It is this yearning and the thirst for knowledge that keeps pushing us all to know more, solve the mysteries and to always push the bar. We continuously seek the meaning of life and existence...

This is what I am trying to make you cognizant about if you aren't already—there is a life cycle in every form, some human and many not. Everything that we see around us has a beginning and an end and merely manifests itself in a new form. There is creation, existence and then destruction. In some weird way, everything in life has a life-cycle of its own.

There will come a time when it will all make sense, and we may be long gone. But what will hopefully remain, are perhaps the relics and archaeological manuscripts to be leveraged or referenced in the future.

Let us now also turn to what is happening with genetic engineering, as that is already beginning to and will have a profound meaning and impact on our lives, not just tomorrow, but for many thousands of years to come. They say that current human beings are normally able to use a maximum of 4% of their brain or mental capacity.

Sure there are always bound to be some exceptional and more realized Souls who can use much more. But, the general population will take a few more hoops and generations to be able to use more of their brains. It's like computer hardware or a phone hardware being built with state of the art technology—it just depends on the software programming to bring in the additional features and special effects to life.

Genetic Engineering

The scientific world is working very hard to try and understand why we are the way we are. To date, they have made tremendous progress in trying to understand the way our chromosomes and our genes work.

This helps in explaining why we look and act the way we do. Today, they can even predict more about our offspring. The deoxy-ribonucleic acid (DNA) has the programming, which guides and defines who we are and why we behave the way we do.

Scientists have been experimenting with decoding our DNA and trying to not only understand but also change or replicate the programming done in our genes. There have been a lot of successes and failures. There are a lot of naysayers and others who say we should not play with nature, while there are others who want to know more about life.

Genetic research continues and one day we will be able to single out each code and DNA strain. For example, we would be able to decode our genetic information to know the person would get cancer at age 41 and after a few years we would be even be able to delete or alter this code so that the person would not get cancer at all.

Would that happen soon? Surely not, but it will one day. Remember we are evolving, our brains our evolving and so is our technology. Genetic Engineering is gaining strength over the past few decades, but in a few hundreds of thousands of years, who knows what kind of advancements will happen.

The genetic (re)design and (re)engineering that we will be able to achieve will enable the creation of entirely new strains of DNA and new or better species of life.

Genetic Engineering—in Life

Today, doctors can check the embryos and determine the sex of the baby. We know that for a lot of childless couples, in vitro fertilization has given so much joy to them and their loved ones. Not only that, either from a donor sperm or egg and once fertilized, they can select from several embryos and choose the embryo they want; a boy or a girl with some known traits—thanks to the advancement of genetic engineering.

Nowadays, we can even detect certain traits of diseases that we understand and can decode, and can even select the embryo that does not have that disease strain in the DNA.

As we perfect this more, I feel we will never have certain diseases going forward. With the evolution cycle and after a few thousand years, we may never get a certain disease again and for successive future generations thus giving rise to that perfect body rid of diseases or at least many of the major and minor ones.

I am sure aging and other aspects are being worked upon by our genetic science community and will yield positive results as well so that a lot of these banes or malaise that the human body must go through will slowly start becoming things of the past.

Remember, these will all happen over the next thousands of years and coupled with our evolution changes, we or at least our future generations will be a formidable species in the universe.

The trick will be the balance of good over evil; as we know with power comes greed, and I see only that coming in the way of all the good that can be achieved. That will possibly come in the way of our progress in the times to come but will also be dealt with by an equal and opposite force. The Creator always keeps the checks and balances in place to not hinder progress for all of us.

Coming back to the topic of genetics, today we can select not just physical traits, but behavioral traits as well. First and with cosmetic surgery, we could select eye or hair color, change our facial and our physical attributes. Today, we are increasingly being able to change the DNA strains in our genes.

We can get genetically modified fruits and vegetable to poultry and other animal life. Research and trial are being done for humans as well—Will there be a person always full of anxiety and depression or will they be a jovial and hearty person?

A few decades ago, when I was in school, there was an essay writing competition: "If parents were made to order, what kind would you choose?" I won an award in that competition as I wrote about robotic parents who could be ordered, especially by the children whose parents had passed away or left them.

Also, how they could have a mommy who never asked them to do homework, but give them ice cream treats whenever they wanted. I could not help but to make a reference as today, that dream and fictional essay is showing more signs of becoming true! We will see a little later as to how this is becoming a reality with the advances in science and technology.

Again, what was inconceivable a generation or two ago, will be a reality after a couple of generations—such is the pace at which the human race, technology and our understanding is evolving and everything around us is too, as we continue to make progress as a race and in our individual lives.

Another famous example of genetic engineering was the cloning of Dolly the sheep. Before that, there were numerous cloning's tried on mice and pigs. Then the genetic engineering community tried cloning a larger animal like a sheep, and Dolly was born, or rather genetically manufactured, or rather manufactured.

Dolly was a huge success as it was the first time a single embryo cell was used to replicate to an entire body. Dolly grew to be a healthy sheep, but died prematurely—not sure why, and not getting into why that happened.

Whatever went wrong, if anything at all, I am sure that our medical science will become much more advanced over the centuries and will be able to program more perfect beings. Dolly left the Earth and a sad scientific community in 2002, but we have been making rapid strides since then, some which we know and some which are going on and under wraps for now.

I can just imagine the world of genetic engineering, and it's accomplishments by 12017—or just 10,000 years from now and again in 102,017, hundred thousand years from now.

In today's world, we hear of Elon Musk and his Neuralink project. What Neuralink is trying to do is create nodes or implants in the human brain. These implants will have their own artificial intelligence with which they can run massive computing on different machines and share the results in order to process vast amounts of information more easily than what we could or would have and create essentially a Cyborg-half machine, half human.
This seems far fetched and coming straight out of a science fiction movie, but I believe this is going to be the reality and something to consider seriously in the years and decades to come.

Physical traits are quite complex in nature. Multiple

genes and genetic codes need to interact with a lot of factors in the environment for the trait to express itself. Thus, quite a bit of research is still required to understand, delineate, select and change complex traits.

However, we are on the track that will soon lead to the ability to make "parent-desired" babies. This would be the era when parents can choose what they would like their offspring to be—an athlete, scientist, actor or whoever by changing certain DNA strains of their upcoming and planned babies.

Once we can break down the genetic order and the genetic codes, we will also be able to make our bodies last longer, avoid diseases and solve a lot of our current challenges and as some of you are thinking—sure, we will give rise to a whole new set of challenges as well!

I believe that in the future, people will be able to create who they want around them. Orphans can choose parents who can be made to order. A child who has lost his parent can recreate them. Parents can recreate their children, friends, family and pets—but it won't be the same! The emotions, feelings, karma and that 6th sense—will all be absent. If you don't mind missing these points, your built replica will be close to filling the void you may have of your loved one.

You should be able to walk into a store or order online from a catalog of profiles for your loved one to be created—ethnicity, color, height, weight, sex, likes, dislikes, language, etc. to be programmed into the gene or the bot. I am not saying whether this is good, or bad, and I don't know if this was to happen this way exactly. But, I do know that this is making things more complicated and challenging.

Welcome to a world of cloned and artificial life!

It's coming, and it will be a reality, starting now for many thousands of years to come! There have been so many movies and so much has been written on this—machines taking over the world and a fight between human intelligence and machine intelligence.

We will take it as it comes. But, given my understan-

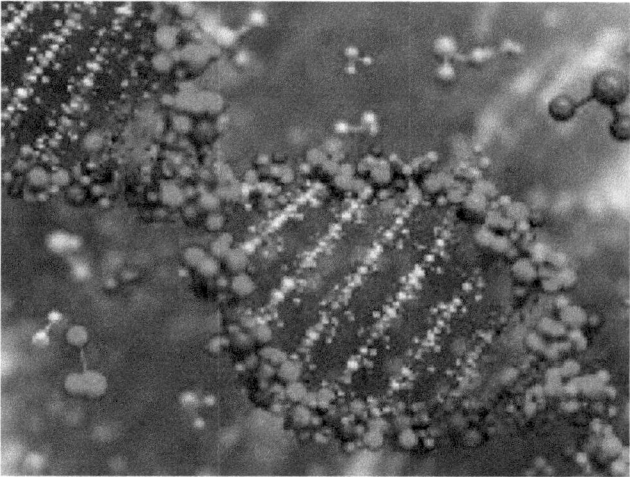

Lincoln, 2005, UN

ding of the whole, I am at peace that something will have the right of way. God can trump any problems. Sure, there will be disturbances and damage on the way but again, is this all staged?

Is this what we are being given to believe in? Is this real? Or, is this a very real-like dream? A stage? Is it a slice of time which is presenting itself to us to act, or react and open new doors based on the choices we make?

I also believe in the distant future we will come to a point where a lot of these gaps in understanding our world and our existence will be addressed. On one hand, we will have a better understanding of our own existence and will evolve as a species.

Science will be more advanced and will be able to help us do a lot of things deemed impossible, also help us in understanding what we would normally defer to the omnipotent.

Science and technology will break barriers where they would help us in understanding the laws of nature through a more mathematical way. It wouldn't be a tussle between spirituality, science and technology, but a mix of both, where science and technology help in understanding and defining spirituality.

We already understand, for example, the laws of physics in our world. Be it gravitational, quantum or nuclear physics, we now know why the planet revolves, why tides are created and why we just don't float around on Earth. Also, the way lighting and water are created—more understanding of science and technology is actually helping us get closer to the secrets of the universe.

CHAPTER SIX

SCIENCE AND TECHNOLOGY
EVOLUTION?

We spoke about gamification in the first chapter, the Soul and its journey, the scriptures and the human evolution. We were touching the technological landscape, but let us now dive deeper in to what is happening in the technology space. We will discuss its impact on our lives and how it can also have an impact on what we are today and where we can be tomorrow.

After all, this is the creation of the human race, which will continue to evolve and try to get us on the road to the supernatural highway of tomorrow!

It started a long time back with the invention of tools—the wheel, planes, trains, the Industrial Revolution and now the Cyber Revolution.

What have we built recently that was not here 50 years ago? We had trains, planes, cars and submarines even back then. We even put a man on the moon with that technology and with those slow, clunky computers. Submarines, nuclear bombs and reactors all existed—so did space travel.

What did not happen then and what has and is happening now is the reach of information and the way we are using the information. Older things are getting better, newer things are getting invented, but the most important aspect is that our lives are changing dramatically.

The good part is that we are able to get more done, but the bad part is in that pretext—we are not having to move much for our needs since they are coming to us. Let us see the evolution of technology—some old and some very new!

The TV, satellite broadcasting, weather and news—instant and accurate reporting, medical science, telecommunications, retail, entertainment, banking, manufacturing, the entire B2B (business to business) and B2C (business to consumer) space, travel, logistics, defense and aerospace, energy and utilities production—all have grown in leaps and bounds.

Many of this was there before, but not at the fast pace and the scale at which it is available, the way the services and products are growing and morphing today.

An example is the way the computer has evolved. We used to have these giant mainframes taking up huge rooms. Today's smartphones take up just the space of your palm but have more computing and storage power than the mainframes of yesterdays. The list goes on and on—we see the evolution of satellites, phones, equipment, tools, automobiles and even buildings.

Internet of Things, sensors, robotics, automation, and neural networks are gaining momentum by the day. Mitsubishi Electric is putting up farms of solar panels in the sky to get raw and uninterrupted solar energy from the Sun and beaming it down to a distribution center on Earth. Then, it would connect to a local grid to power your homes, super markets, cars and shops.

Another example is a program in the North Sea to develop energy from renewable sources using the constant force of the waves going back and forth. They have created huge platforms with large dongs hanging down from them. These dongs move back and forth when the wave comes and hits them.

The kinetic energy of the waves is then transferred to the dongs and converted to mechanical energy and finally into electrical energy for human consumption. There are many examples of projects in conception or advanced stages that can change the way we live and work tomorrow.

We know companies like Google and Uber are trying to put driverless cars on the roads. This would end the notion and need for owning cars and provide a car as a service to get from one point to another.

The business model is hinged on the point that this would be a much more affordable price and save you your money once you weigh in all the factors that come with owning a car—fuel, registrations, maintenance, wear and tear, parts replacement and loss of capital value.

We are rapidly seeing advancement in technology in different spheres of our lives in industrial, electronics, cyber and space evolution. In fact, we see the greatest evolution in the armed forces.

A global arms race is virtually inevitable if any major military power pushes ahead with Artificial Intelligence (AI) weapons development; the group cautioned at the International Joint Conferences on AI in Buenos Aires on July 28th, 2015.

"The stakes are high," the letter said. "Autonomous weapons have been described as the third revolution in warfare, after gunpowder and nuclear arms," and thus started the campaign to stop killer robots. Other notable tech figures, including Apple's Co-

Samiksha S., 2016

Founder, Steve Wozniak, and Google Deep Mind CEO, Demis Hassabis, are also signatories to the letter.

Autonomous weapons—think pistol toting terminators, smart vehicles with mounted machine guns and self-piloted bomber drones—aren't just the stuff of science fiction anymore. As the letter notes, some weapons systems are "Feasible within years, not decades."

Elon Musk and Stephen Hawking are discerned individuals who have drawn attention to the threat we face if robots were deployed in the military. Even for defense forces as that would set off a great arms race of a different and very lethal kind.

You would not be able to kill them, and they would increasingly become more powerful and have powers to self-heal and become almost indestructible. Whichever country or group that possesses such robots, would be feared and rule the world.

Elon has hinted at how powerful robots can be.

Once connected to servers, they can instantly monitor traffic in Beijing, somebody's health record in Philadelphia, see a person crossing between platforms on Oxford station using the CCTV cameras there, monitor a car race going on in Dubai or oversee a murder happening in Delhi.

Movies like *Rogue One* all detail the future where humans would co-exist with machines and with beings from other planets. To some, this might seem fictitious and impossible, and to some, it might feel very real.

Few of the examples coming to us over the next few years are:

1. *Google, like clouds transporting water, is using balloons to transmit wireless Internet from the sky directly to your home. Pilot projects have started in select US cities.*

2. *We spoke about the driverless car pilots that Google and Uber are working on.*

3. *We already have cell phones that can do wireless charging and all these technologies*

will get better over the years! One day we will not require a single wire in our homes!

4. *The way we shop and use our cards will change. Soon our mobile phone will have icons for our driving license, medical cards, shopping and travel cards, airlines and hotels, pharmacies and malls. The traditional plastic card will be a thing of the past very soon. This is already starting to happen and will be a reality very soon!*

5. *All fridges will have weight sensors to detect that the family is low on milk and will automatically dial the local grocery store to order and it will be delivered to your doorstep. You would have an online and secure account with the store, and you will just have to authorize the request your refrigerator made. It will free up your grocery store trip time, effort and fuel to do mundane tasks like that.*

6. *The same will go for you washing the kitchen and other areas of your home. Shopping, Travel and tourism—everything is going to*

go digital and become revolutionized in ways unthinkable even just five years back.

7. *Intelligent buildings, roads, dams, bridges, homes, cars and appliances will be the future. We have already started going in that direction with the wired and digital world, and this will start becoming more of the norm, not just in the Tier 1 cities, but also in Tier 2 and 3 countries and cities as well.*

Till now, we used to connect our appliances by wires, travel by road, rail or air and have many things connected through a medium. In my view, the future would be focused on removing the medium; wires, pipes, pipelines, roads, and highways will be a thing of the past in a few decades, if not sooner.

Space and time travel would be the order of the day! Even the very way we think the points are connected will change.

The medium that connects the two endpoints will see a tectonic and paradigm shift in the way they used to join or connect. A new technology or innovation will come in which would break the traditional ways to connect devices, people, assets and cities.

Remember the movie Star Trek where Captain James Kirk of the USS Enterprise says, "Spock, beam me up!" This fantasy and science fiction movie is what the next phase of life will chase to achieve.

The first phase was to build cars, the second to build automatic and self-driving cars, the third would be to have flying cars. The next phase would be to remove road and sky travel and jump time dimensions, so you get beamed up, or get from place A to place B, without a medium or traditional route that we used in the past. This may take a few thousand years, but it is my strong belief that we will get there one day!

We must! The non-existence of this kind of technology will not be an option, given the challenges that humankind will face in the centuries to come. In a few thousand years, the Earth will no longer be habitable. The population would have grown multi-fold and the strain it will put on our

Loon Company, 2017

natural resources would be so much that there will not be enough for all.

How do I see the world of tomorrow? Very fascinating and exciting! I see buildings, which have rotating apartments and floors so that your living room can face the sun from morning to evening.

Also, I see movable buildings that move on a track in such a way that a consortium of buildings can all move and every resident can pass along the seashore for a while. Depending on how much "sea-view" time they have paid for up to a predefined time limit, giving more people in different buildings access to the beautiful ocean view.

This would remove the constraint of only a few homes enjoying the sea view. In the future, we would have the floors rotating so that every part of the building gets to enjoy the view and so also the other buildings, which otherwise would not have had the chance.

I see food, medicine and water being created at will and at any point for everyone, whether you are in the middle of the sea, desert, hill or jungle. I see robots working hand in hand with us and helping us in our everyday lives—cooking food, cleaning the house, building roads, bridges, buildings and space shuttles; in fact even building more robots and machines.

In fact, I feel in the world of tomorrow everything will come to you—your office, your mall, your grocery store, your cinema hall, your school, bank, post office, your court, library and so many other day-to-day essentials.

Some are already using our smartphones, but I feel that the AI/AR/VR (virtual reality/) areas are going to make giant and rapid strides to change the definition and the meaning of getting places and people to us.

This could initially have opposition regarding jobs and markets having to rebalance themselves, but as we have seen in the past, the induced problems create other opportunities regarding monitoring, security, advanced sensors, programming, parts, communications and other boundless opportunities.

I see less disease, lower mortality rates and huge opportunities for all of us. Not just on Earth, but beyond and onto other planets and moons as we move forward in our journey of life!

The life of tomorrow is going to have a different meaning as we evolve. We will have holograms of ourselves created and which would never die and could be there when needed, even when the physical body has died already. Our hologram and program would have learned our behaviors, emotions, relations and our other points would be able to be projected at will. It could be someone that we want to speak to in difficult times.

For example, a child wanting to connect with their deceased parent, the hologram could help guide your child with learning and teachings with ways of consolation. Giving a lecture, performance, medical or mechanical operation in another part of the world, or on a different planet that we have discovered or are inhabiting, would become so much easier and life-like! Is it hard to imagine Wimbledon being telecast to other planets far away?

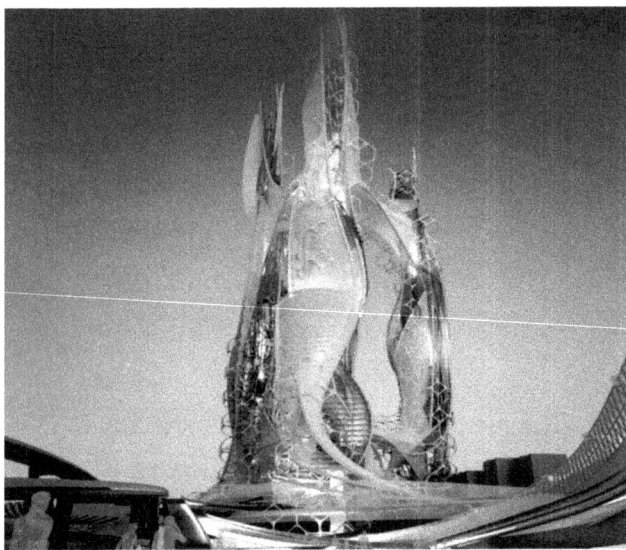

Vincent Berg, 2013

Then you will have the race of cyborgs, which will be running amok. The cyborgs will be half humans and half machines. As we read earlier, the first steps towards that is beginning (referencing: the Neuralink project), and we will soon have another race, which will be the extension to ours.

The brain will be ours, while the limbs and other parts of the body will be mechanical, but controlled by our brain. We will have fewer people with bone and muscle issues. An example of this is a mutilated body in an accident. We are already seeing bionic limbs being implanted to help us.

With a living brain and mind, the other parts of the body can easily be replaced with mechanical parts —legs, hands, fingers, eyes, heart and other body parts. We have seen an example and a fictitious character by the name of Mr. Spock in the movie *Star Trek*.

As we advance, there will be many places in our lives where it would be better to have a cyborg, or humanoid, instead of just robots or a human being. Even a few years ago, this would have been described as fiction. Even today, lots of people will have doubt on how this would all work out.

As we have seen in the past, the same things thought of as impossible, can become a reality in a few generations. That is why I am saying we are entering the next phase of our lives, a life form previously thought unattainable, in *Life 2.0*.

The advancements happening in space tourism, genetic engineering, artificial intelligence, robots, medicine, quantum physics, communication, energy and the changes that are coming to insurance and banking, retail, manufacturing, healthcare, travel and tourism, and resources are going to be so interesting.

I wish I could be there to see it all unfold! The only way is to be like time or God—some energy or form, which is limitless, endless and omnipresent everywhere.

True, we will probably start living a few hundred years, and the average lifespan in 202017 may be around 250 years. We are already averaging around

90 years for a lifespan in some of the countries. So it is not too far fetched to think that with all the technological advances, we should be able to at least double our current life spans.

There is enough data and information available publicly, and from the United Nations, that shows the way we have grown on this planet for the last 200 years–from a billion in the year 1800 A.D. to 7+ billion in 2017. What this means is that in 200 years, we have grown about seven times—you see where I am going with this? We are growing at an exponential rate in just a slice of time.

My personal projection is that we will hit 10 billion in the next two generations or by 2117, and we will hit 20 billion by the year 2217. By the year 3017, or a thousand years more, there won't be enough space for us to live on this planet!

There will be a lot of competition for our natural resources—land, water, oil and minerals. There will hardly be any forests, deserts or ravines left to inhabit and much of the animal life will probably have to be phased out to make way for us humans.

Vincent Berg, 2013

Some will become extinct, as they will have less and less places to live. Their habitats will be destroyed, and as the jungles around the world go, the climates and weather patterns will change as well. The poles will most likely not exist in the way we know them today.

The atmospheric currents will change the season patterns and will create havoc for all the Earth's species, from insects, birds and fish to other animals. There will be a great struggle for habitable land. The price of land will be astronomically high, lots of social unrest will abound and there will probably be many wars between nations.

The good part is that as this happens, there will be consortium or alliances of nations and maybe even consolidations to solve these problems. There will be more social revolutions and wars as we fight for space to live on; survival and existence will be the No.1 priority. Genetic evolution will play out again —survival of the fittest.

While that happens, our science and technology will figure out a way for humans to live on the moon or some habitable planet.

We have already seen some distant planets show signs of being able to support a life form such as ours. So, we will probably put a dome of oxygenated air on hundreds of miles on one of these planetary bodies and create water, food and other essential things for our survival and existence.

We cannot expect water to be available on every other planetary body. But, we know the technology of mixing hydrogen and oxygen to create water and that is what we must setup—a water generation plant up there. Mind you with evolution and environments, our bodies will adapt as well.

We will also start having cities and buildings built on mezzanine type levels. Streets and highways will be built on top of one another creating a few levels. The same would be for rail tracks, runways and other means of transportation.

We will all have more authorized levels to fly in the sky—for flying cars to government aerial vehicles, passenger aerial cars and buses, and those with zcategory—just like we have different radio frequency bands, some allowed for the public and some for the police and government.

They say necessity is the mother of invention!

Earlier, we spoke of the cyborgs. Slowly the advancement in medical science and genetic engineering, robotics and IOT (Internet of Things) will come to a crossroad where we will start producing some very sleek mechanical robots, or even robots that are like humans (not cyborgs)—these would have all the systems built in- waste management systems, neural networks, transmission networks, electrical, charging and back up networks, sight, hearing and speech networks, and they would not need to rest, sleep, eat or drink.

There could come a time where these would be a very powerful force to leverage and contend with.

They could be called Humanoids (machines which are like humans), some of our movies reference them, but whatever the name, the machine race will exist. This is not a figment of my imagination, nor am I having an overdose on movies, this is happening as we speak. Let us see a few examples where this is beginning to happen:

Let's take the case of robots now helping us in a shopping mall in Japan. Instead of meeting a human assistant, you're greeted by this robot dressed in a kimono and doing the customary bow. The robots like 'Pepper' are close to reaching the level of human intelligence. At 120 cm tall and nearly 30 kilos in weight, these machines analyze gestures, expressions and even the tone of voices.

You can ask the robot, "Where is cosmetics located?" and the robot will find out the GPS co-ordinates where you are standing, map it in the catalog of products in the store and direct you politely in the right direction.

These robots are proving to be very popular. One reason for that was the emotion-reading function. They can understand and read expressions, overlay that with speech recognition to understand the context and provide the correct response to the person. Situational context will be an area that will see a vast amount of technological improvement.

We already see the success of drones. Soon, we are going to have automated police cars and motorcycles patrolling our streets by the end of this century. These are very exciting times, to say the least! But, have no doubt in your mind as to what is coming!

The movement of robots and AI are not just in the western world and some of the advanced countries.

Take the case of Sandy in India for example. Sandy is a 5-ft tall, blue-colored Humanoid who is highly intelligent and has immense potential.

Sandy can warn you if your house is on fire, can play your favorite videos for you, read stories to your children, play chess with them and remind your elderly parents to take their medication on time. She can tell you if you will meet traffic on your way to the office and when you come back home, she will ask about your day and respond accordingly.

Virtual or augmented reality will be the thing of the future. Right now, as we discussed in the first chapter, it's been a huge success in the gaming industry. Already, we see how virtual reality is going to be the way we shop in the future: sit on our couches at home, put on virtual reality glasses, go throughout the mall, the aisles, select what we need and checkout.

The same goes for movies, taking trips to the Swiss Alps, a tour of Stonehenge, Machu Pichu, the Taj Mahal and all the other tourist destinations, all by sitting in your home. As for the near future, all eyes are on the 2020 Tokyo Olympics—where the robots could potentially help foreign visitors.

We now understand and can predict certain behaviors of the universe and the world around us better than we could a mere 100 years ago. We can predict storm systems, plot the trajectory and paths of comets, gauge earthquakes and tsunamis, studying the bursting of stars and the creation of black holes.

Our understanding of physics, chemistry and biology is helping us understand more about the way matter reacts, forms and transforms itself. We are similarly able to do the same for energy, the way it is formed, transforms and can be used.

The ability to measure distances in the galaxies and our universe, as well as understanding how it is governed is getting better by the day. This is just the beginning!

I feel every second represents a slice of the universe. We or rather our souls can move between the time-slices and manifest itself in a context with related folks around. Based on our Soul and karma, we can move between these time-slices and take a form - that of an animal, human or higher order being, an innate object or a plant or stone for example. It's like frames in a movie reel.

Say Universe 1 has a zillion time-slices or time stamps. We can go through these time stamps and evolve and move from being a rock to a living being to a human or higher species. On the other hand, and especially when our loving universe decides to contract and self-destruct, we can change to a time-slice of another universe and an altogether different context/setting again. Okay, let's not get bogged down by all this and see what we should do today whether the above is true or not.

As we transition from Life 1.0 to *Life 2.0*, our understanding of this beautiful world will largely get enhanced, and we will start appreciating and understanding the meaning and the reasons of our universe and its laws.

Knowledge is power and the more knowledgeable we are, the more we can understand, create and change the laws that work around us. It will be like changing our genetic code, but we will fully have to understand the ramifications and only then be an instrument to bring about that change.

A saying that comes to mind is *A little knowledge is a dangerous thing*. We must be wise, and make any changes only once we fully understand what and all that is going on around us.

CHAPTER
SEVEN

THE CONNECTION AND THE
MEANING

Do you see what I am driving at? I speak of gaming, then our religious scriptures, the concept of the Soul, science and technological innovations and some of you may wonder what are these various topics pointing to and how are they all related to each other? Each of these is a world by itself and has a universe of its own.

There is no way these different worlds can intersect. Or, can they? And that is what I am trying to say; they all aren't worlds of their own with no intersection. In fact, I believe nothing exists without a connection with the other, and they all are deeply connected.

There will be avatars, holograms, spawning of life and machine life that will change our thoughts on what is possible. Which in turn will start stretching and pushing the limits of technology, as we know it at that point in time.

We will transcend to an existence not previously thought possible. It is not that spirituality will be a different path and of its own, and that genetic engineering or technology will develop on a different trajectory.

In the process of advancing genetic engineering, creating humanoids and cyborgs, we will soon see a convergence and an overlap happening, and one will not be possible without the other.

A point in time will come when a lot of the fantasy world, what our holy scriptures have taught us, the teachings of our spiritual masters, advances in technology and innovation, as well as the journey of the Soul, will reach a tipping point and will all join and live in co-existence with each other. All this will converge and conjoin and start making more sense—some day!

The problem is that today there are a lot of naysayers, as none of this is usually seen, proven or understood. Those against God say, "Who knows if God exists?" The people who believe in God say, "Everything is as per Him and His guidance only." Some will say, "Humans can never create life, only God can." Then there are others who will say, "God had billions of years to his credit, while humans have had a few thousand years only."

Give the human race a couple of million years, and then that will be a good yardstick to measure what they have achieved. Then, the other side will say, "Whatever the human, cyborg or humanoid race achieves is all because of the human brain, which was created by God."

There would be a school largely believed and followed by the religious community, yet another by the scientific community and there would be others that would be either confused or not sure of what is correct. The debate would go on and on until a time will come albeit in a few hundreds of thousands of years when the human brain would have evolved to such an extent that some of those evolved species would actually be in the kingdom of the Gods.

It will only be then that these debates and different viewpoints will all cease as our intellect and understanding unravel these deep secrets of our universe and help us to find the answers to many of these questions that we have time and again.

I would say while these debates go on for an extended period of time, the advancements that would happen—along with the challenges and opportunities that all this would bring in—would bring a lot of these varying paths to converge and bring in a lot of peace and contentment of who we are and what we are meant to be.

In the grand scheme of things, we cannot rush to conclusions, or understand things at this given point and draw a decision based on the very limited

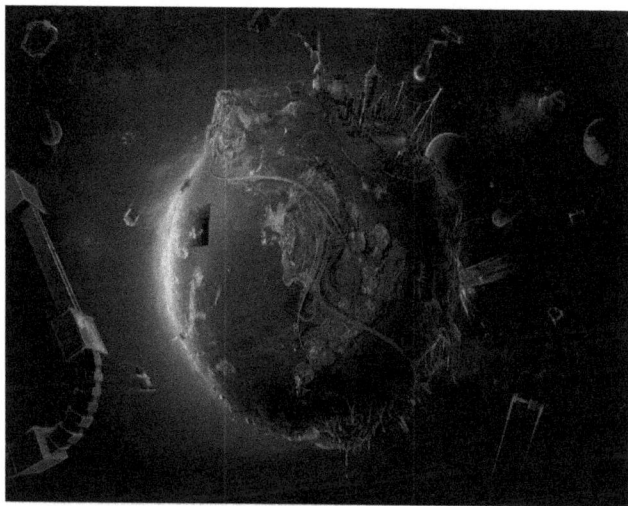

Plochu Systému, 2017

knowledge and understanding we have today of our world and the universe.

There are lots of cosmic laws, which will have to be understood over a period of time. For now, I feel you should adopt whatever you feel is right, as long as that is for the good and without harming anybody or anything and it gives you inner peace and happiness. Let the time come—it may not be in this birth or current day setting, but it might be, depending on your karma.

But, the day all these points can be explained, they will meet and everything will make more sense that day. That day may be different for everyone. Not everyone will understand at the same time, but one day we all will as we progress in our spiritual, material and technological lives.

We know that the laws of physics, gravity, quantum physics, chemistry and biology, are all governed by some unexplained laws. Why is each snowflake so distinct in the way it is? There are the laws that govern us all and in all spheres of our lives.

We need to look around and open our inner eyes and intellect to see them. The way the flowers bloom, the way the seasons happen, the way the waves ebb and flow; everything is harmoniously dancing to that cosmic tune.

You should immerse yourself in the tune and feel enchanted by it. You don't have to do or achieve anything–it's all scripted, and you are playing a part in it. In my earlier years, I used to think if I sit down and do nothing and if I don't get up and do my exams, how can I pass... let alone get a good grade?

With time, I have now understood that because of the way I am programmed, I cannot sit and let things go by. The sense of control in me will be so strong that I will feel challenged and compelled to act and achieve.

I have realized that a lot of things that happened out of the blue were meant to happen. Whether I call it a stroke of luck or being at the right place at the right time—all of these things happen without me being in control of the other situations or people. I might have opened the right door or have been led to it.

Just like in the car racing game in chapter 1, the road develops depending on the turns we take. The track is automatically and randomly generated based on the turn or choice we make.

In those games, as we take turns and different routes, the road, the background and the silhouettes change accordingly, and we go on. Remember that the start and the end are the only two points defined. Similarly, our lives and futures will change with the choices we make and the doors we choose to open.

There are choices we must make every moment, voluntary or involuntarily—that is what makes the game and life more enriching. There will be massive changes to Genetic and Human Engineering, natural progress of evolution and the massive strides that humans will create to develop robots and machines.

The future will have more intelligent earthly beings. I don't know if they will be called humans or remain humane, or if they will be called something else like Earth beings. Their thought process and powers will be far more superior to anything we have known. It's just like asking a monkey to make sense of it all. Can it really?

Can you ask a child to comprehend what is happening in the world—how can the poor thing? That child's brain has not developed enough to make sense of anything apart from parents, school and friends.

Just because we have a little intellect now, we shouldn't think that we have reached our full potential. There is a lot for our brains to evolve and harness. Give it a few million years and our, or the new Earth-race's, brains will be able to think and do much more that we could ever imagine.

It's the difference between the monkeys and us, only so much more; just as we are so much more advanced than a monkey, so will the new species be far more evolved!

We have seen how the Earth is going to be destroyed one day, or at least become inhabitable; the solar

Nasa, 2016

system and others will implode just like the way they were created. But, humans and/or the Earth-race will move on. The journey will be different than the world today. However, the important point is that it will go on.

You may feel sad at the thought of the Earth blowing up one day, as this is what we call our home. You may think that we will become a secondary species and go from being the rulers of the planet, but remember that we are not who we really are, but are just playing a part.

Our names could be John, Ismail, Rohan, Oscar, Satvinder, Rita, Naaz, Ramatu, Helen or Svetlana, but that is just for this birth. We will possibly move into each other roles in our next birth, or go somewhere totally different. What I am saying is– thoughts, actions, words and desires leading to karma and that in turn giving the guide to our Souls on what to be and where to go next in our spiritual lives.

Then there is a grander plan in store for you and every one of us; we are merely following the cosmic rules.

The cosmic rules flow throughout the universe and beyond. The assumption here is that there are many other universes. But, for a Soul to travel to a point in this creation and in a certain time/location and dimension, there is a law and an equation to achieve that.

If you were to send the Soul as if it was a postal mail, you would need the coordinates of the next body it will inherit. This can best be described in what I feel are in 10 dimensions.

We are trying to mimic nature and the creation as best as we can. The way our aerial vehicles and submersible vehicles work today are is if they are trying to mimic birds and fish. Even the robots are trying to mimic the human body.

I believe that as we go about inventing and creating robots, cyborgs or Humanoids, we have to give them a universal and unique cosmic code and context. Without that, how would we differentiate between a robot called X001 on Earth and another called the same X001 on the moon or Mars?

Also, as we go toward creation and procreation, for all of us to be uniquely identifiable, to be relevant, conscious and alive in our current cosmic context and understand the movements from one dimension to another, we need to understand and comprehend these 10 axes:

1. *X-axis*

2. *Y-axis*

3. *Z-axis – Starts giving the depth.*

4. *S-axis – Sensory organs – Gives sight, hearing, smell, taste and touch. You can feel you are poking someone and you are getting into the z-axis, but also getting a pushback/pressure giving it a more real feeling.*

5. *N-axis – Nervous system – Which is the neural networks running in the body culminating in the brain to make sense of it all and the inputs from all the axes.*

6. *E-or ESP axis – Extra sensory perception or the 6th sense or your sub consciousness; also called your conscience.*

7. *T-axis – Time axis – Which denotes all these senses, body and mind, but in which time dimension?*

8. *L-Axis – The Location axis – Which gives the body, the mind, the time axis and the location–which planet, star, situation–palace or the footpath you will be born and raised in.*

9. *K-axis – The Karma axis – Our deeds, based on which we can attain a certain T-L (Time and Location) axis co-ordinate in the overall cosmic frame.*

10. *A-axis – Astral axis – This being the most important one–this is what governs the entry of the Soul into the body or the moving out of it and the next address/body it has to flow into – kind of a master key to all this grandeur.*

Our next generation robots must get these axes

right, or else they will not be able to mimic the grand creation. The day we can break the code into and replicate these axes, we can put a human being, a cyborg or a living robot into the universal cycle and its mix—of moving between time warps and dimensions, from one body to another and from one solar system of a galaxy to another.

To do that and get it all right, we will probably take a few million years. By then, I believe some of us will have learned to breathe life into these forms that we create and energize their A (Astral) axis. Life that is not mechanical, electrical or nuclear but more as a natural life form that will be possible to create.

This won't be by us, but our future genetically advanced brethren who would be far more advanced than any one of us are or can imagine. This will also rest the point that humans can't create life. Yes, humans in the current times cannot but an evolved, and genetically more advanced species and a derivative of the human form will possibly be able to one day.

There will be a handful of folks at any given point in time who are realized and who can always do this in any generation including today, but I am speaking of a more repeatable and predictable outcome at scale. Of course, and for now, the first thing is to try flying at the speed of light or create the cosmic warps for space and time travel. This should be done so that we can understand the length and breadth of this universe and get to know other civilizations and learn from their science and technology as well.

There will come a day and time when we can merge all these axes together and breathe life into a being. The day we do so, we will be close to creating a DNA-cloned or DNA-new being with a Soul and life which is not just mechanical, or electrical, and following instructions and commands but be just like any one of us.

How would the Soul of these beings be created and how would it then weave with all the other aspects of life? This becomes a big question, and I must say I don't have an answer to that. I do not claim to know it all, and I am also on the journey like so many of you.

I am trying to find answers myself, and I will write again if I do have answers to some of these questions and as I learn more… if I am destined to learn more in this birth that is.

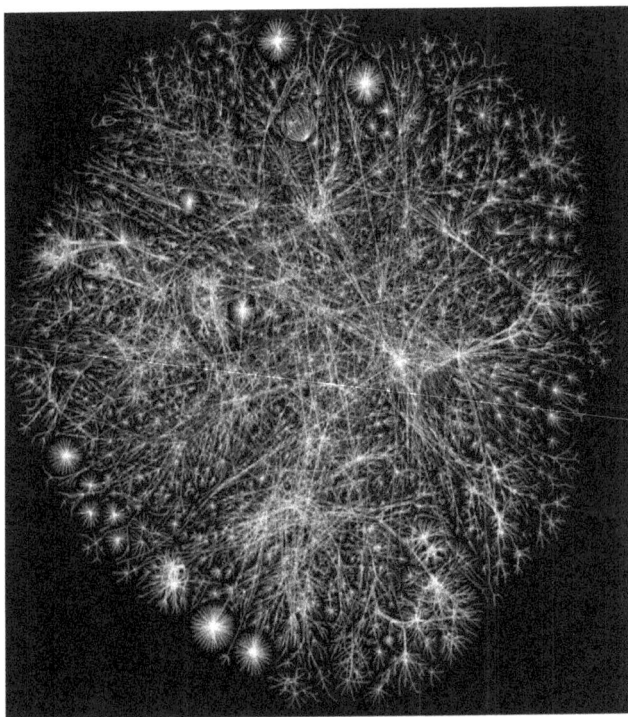

Emily Anne Epstein , 2015

CHAPTER EIGHT

SUMMING IT ALL UP–LIFE 2.0!

Shakespeare has said, "All the world's a stage." We come in when our part in the play begins, play the part and leave the stage. So, do all the characters in a story.

Earlier on, we heard about Jim Morrison speaking of breaking through to the other side. We also looked at what The Matrix was trying to say about the two worlds—physical and astral.

The Bible says this about cremation, "By the sweat of your face you shall eat bread, till you return to the ground, for out of it you were taken; for you are dust and to dust you shall return."

We are made of the dust of the Earth, and that is what we turn back into after we die. But, this is talking about the body and not the Soul. The spirit of man will live beyond the grave, but not with the body.

For those who have died, they will be joined back up with their bodies at the resurrection of the dead, and they will either be with the Lord or in eternal torment based on their karma. Through this book, I wanted to bring about a few points in your mind and express my viewpoint towards what could be the truth and the meaning of Life.

But, to do that, understanding the scriptures, technological and human evolutions, the concept of the Soul and other points were very important to give a well-rounded view and perspective.

I would first like to thank my readers. There are bound to be questions, different perspectives and understandings, and maybe some misunderstan-

Martina Atiriamin, 2003

dings and that is okay. All I would like to earnestly and sincerely request everyone is to make peace with one another.

Do not judge people by their country, origin, religion or faith, and most of all do not harm any being. We don't know a whole lot of what is going on in our world and universe. But, it seems like the one way to succeed on Earth and give ourselves a better chance in our next births, and definitely our future generations, is to love and spread love, be compassionate and be humane.

Bloodshed, killings and wars are not the answers to the immense problems we are about to face in the years to come—they will just increase our problems and divide us further.

While writing this, I also realize that I cannot change anything. I am doing what I was meant to do. You and others will do what is destined. What must happen, will happen and what has happened has already happened. We are all here for a reason, and we will pass on from this stage after we have played our parts. Others will come and play our part and we will play theirs. But do remember, we have a little leeway in making the choice and bringing about change. Destiny does dictate your life, but you have a window of opportunity to change your destiny.

We were created and given the situations we operate and live in because of our karma and our desires. But we can start to bring about that change by starting to bring about that change within ourselves. By being a better, loving and being a more compassionate human being irrespective of what and how others behave towards us.

Our smile should be able to change the World, but the way the World reacts should not be able to change our smile!

Also, there might be this question—Why do we have to pass away from Earth and our loved ones? Why do flowers have to bloom and die? Why are plants, pets, animals, in fact, all living and non-living things created and destroyed?

With what I mentioned in the last few chapters,

I think the answer is that nothing is created or destroyed—everything exists and just manifests itself in different forms; a continuous cosmic rearrangement!

It gives us all a chance to live our dreams, fulfill them and move on. It's a journey of the self and self-realization. It's a constant cosmic pattern of creation, existence and then fading away and merging with the bigger cosmic parts.

There is truly no beginning or end. It is only the beginning and an end of a form just like a snowflake. It gets generated, is there for a while and then changes. So do we and all whom we love.

With evolution, each and every upcoming generation becomes stronger and better, giving path to a better species, different surroundings, a different context and a different meaning. In the absence of all of this, if we all were immortal, had the same friends, enemies, co-workers, relatives and society, things would start to become a little uninteresting—perhaps.

Sometimes you could see monotony settling in a group of friends. After many parties or meetings, you know almost everything about each other, and there is nothing more to know or discuss. Putting in a new character and the experience or discussion points he or she brings in, changes the discussion and the atmosphere starts getting more charged and enriching. Similarly, the cycle of life and death and the introduction of new characters in our lives just spices up the entire creation and brings in something new and fresh.

One of the important universal and cosmic rules is change! It is this change that brings about the freshness and the variety in the space—be it a stage, time dimension or a situation.

If there is no change, it starts to become boring. Perhaps that is why God created this cycle of coming into the world and then leaving. Come with your memory wiped out and leave with your memory wiped out as well; Come into the world with nothing and leave with nothing; from zero to zero, from dust to dust, from a spark to a spark or a speck of energy back to a speck of Energy.

We know that a child or a newborn has no recollection of anything and is like a brand new person. We also saw that in extreme circumstances, some of them recollect their past. But, for most folks, a newborn baby has no recollection of anything and starts life afresh. The soul of this baby does know, but this gift of the present life has been bestowed or earned by the Soul to do something that would change the course of its life and make an impact on the others that it interacts with, in a good or bad way!

When we lose a loved one, we feel very pained and depressed, and almost everyone asks why? Why did this happen and more specifically why did we have to go through this? There are two paths to dealing with this:

1. *Don't have anything that gives you that pain—no possessions, no attachments to anything, person, place or thing. Be like the Gautama Buddha!*

2. *Accept that it is a part of life and there is a grand design behind this all and move on.*

While the former is easier said than done, the latter is difficult and tears your heart. Gautama Buddha, or Siddhartha as he was known when he was a King, saw the worldly sufferings of disease, old age and death. He relinquished his kingdom, cut ties with his family and went into the forests to try to uncover the truth.

Most of our spiritual leaders and masters ask us not to be attached to anything or anyone, as an end is inevitable and with that comes the grief of separation. Attachment creates pain, and we should try to love but be detached from any person, place or thing—simple, but very difficult.

Life is a constant cycle of creation-destruction, creation-destruction, almost like a child building blocks, breaking them and making it again—a relentless pursuit of the perfection till a time when it is so perfect that it is almost Godly! Then, you stop and go to build another—and the cycle continues.

Just as a game has different levels and versions, we are also moving towards a different plane and with different versions of us. As we make decisions and the opportunities in front of us change, so do the characters and people we meet that are around us. As the games have different versions and as they become better and more realistic, don't we as well?

Several questions come to the mind:

1. *On a timescale of 10 million years, how have we fared?*

2. *How have we upgraded and what roles do we play?*

3. *Do we get to play only as a human being on Earth, or can we move to another planet or star and play another part?*

4. *Is the world all we know, or is this just a tiny speck in this grand cosmic play?*

5. *Is God a higher species or form, or is He a Father and ultimate one?*

6. *Is He there, and does He have an entire government to support Him with ministers,*

local zodiac and astral heads?

7. Will we ever know?

8. When will we know?

9. Do we need to know?

There is so much happening in the technological, medical and other scientific worlds, but is there a place where the learning and the solutions from science cross over to the spiritual world? Is there a way our technology and the digital world works hand in glove with our spiritual world?

While we speak about our digital lives, can it be that what we create is merely a portal and a gateway to a much deeper and mysterious background of the actual and spiritual life? I think so.

As we've seen earlier, my honest opinion is the answer to all this will come to me when I am ready for it. Till then, there is no point in going crazy and trying to answer these questions. We have a life and let's make the best of it. Be good and spread love.

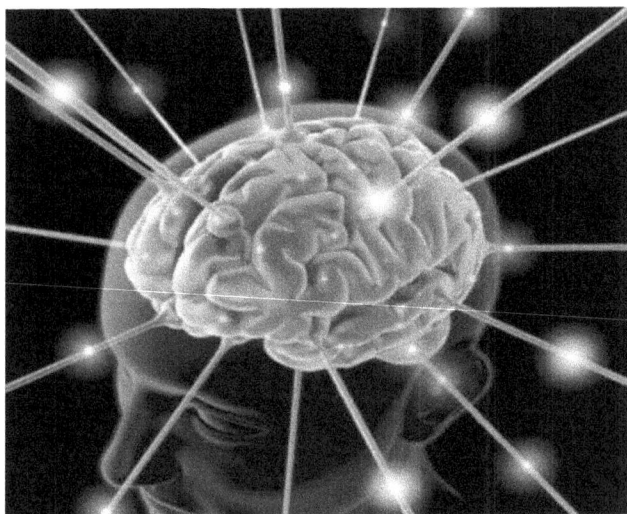

Yashraj Kakkad, 2015

This life is a test and a present. Lead it well, and one will get a chance to climb the spiritual ladder. Have the questions and realize that you will pull the Cosmos and its celestial frequencies to you, but it might come to you in due time. Hence, don't get paranoid with the questions.

Be aware of the larger design, but be at peace within yourself and love; We are often asked to meditate, read our scriptures and follow our rituals—all these give a meaning and a sense of fulfillment in our lives. They try to bring that inner peace and strength, a lifeline to latch on to, whenever our lives start getting shaky. There is something, or someone, looking after us and after our interests.

Remember, we need to settle our account in this birth and maybe a few others until our karmic account is net positive with good deeds. Until then, we cannot proceed further in our celestial journey. So love and spread love and get rid of hatred and crime.

Till then, we need to continue this journey called life. In the first phase, it took the first few million years for the human beings to be formed is what I call Life 1.0. This was the time when we learned to make tools that help us.

We are in the second and next phase and will be for a few more million years till we max out on Earth and become a very advanced species, which is what I call *Life 2.0*. This is the time when we make Humanoids, which will be almost like humans and will help, and in some cases, replace us. Life 1.0 was when the human race got created.

Life 2.0 will be our quest to create as well as it would be the era where there would be the next genetic split where humans would continue, but a more advanced race would get created and would continue for the next few million years. Life 1.0 was more of a self-discovery and learning phase– there were lots of questions and lesser answers.

Life 2.0 would be where we understand enough and start using some laws and cosmic order into creating new lives. There would still be questions, but there would be more answers and understanding available of the whys and what's of our universe.

I cannot foretell what Life 3.0 and 4.0 will look like, but I guess when we get to that, the lines will blur between God Almighty and the generation that exists that day. It will probably not be just us but folks from other celestial origins as well. It is impossible to predict what our future generations will be and the technology and spiritual advancement that will happen a million years from now.

That is thinking too much and too far ahead. This would all be true if there was no change in the ecosystem and the world we live in for another few million years. Is that possible?

The possibilities are endless! We could be visited by another alien civilization. We may have the technology to go out into the universe and discover other civilizations. Wars between the galaxies could happen, as I can only imagine that not all of them will be friendly with the human species and our settlements.

There could be a natural change, like an asteroid or planet changing due to another cosmic rule like the quasars and black holes. What I do know is that our Sun is going to likely be a black hole many billion years from now and would just suck in all the planets including Earth.

Hence finding settlements outside of our solar system is not just far-fetched, but would be a necessity for the sake of the existence of our race and we will all have to move on.

Some of us, including the animals that exist, will not be able to make it. But, what is important is that the essence of human kind and life moves on.

Wow! My small human head spins as I think, write and try to comprehend all this. While several questions come to my mind, I fully realize that I cannot and am not empowered to live until that time, see all this unfold and make a change to these happenings.

However, what I am indeed empowered to do is to feel blessed, to feel His power and the forces that surround me and that are there inside me and that are governing my existence and paving the path forward for me. I am empowered to feel content and happy with my family, friends and society.

I have the power to bring in and exercise a little more love to the people I come across and that are around me, knowing that this is the only way to get change for the better.

Again, this is the way I see the world around me. You could agree or disagree with me, and that is fine. But, I would consider this book to be a success if I can make anyone see the bigger meaning to our existence and our lives.

I would get the greatest satisfaction if I can stop even one person who is going to act in hate, out of greed, lust or any negative passion. Hopefully, after reading this book, it would make that person think, stop and not commit a sin or a negative act— against God, our own world and it's inhabitants or mankind.

Many of us make mistakes in our lives that we regret later. The reason I brought out these different facets of our lives was to make sure that the person realizes the grandeur of everything around us and knows the meaning of it all.

We are all connected and part of the same universe, energy flow and creation because we are all manifestations and instantiations of one universal being or state of existence.

We should always stop for a second and think, who is the other person in front of "us" (not you and I, but our two connected Souls), what are we trying to do to that person, what are we trying to achieve and do we fully comprehend what is it that we are trying to do and achieve?

Is any hate or vengeance or ego really needed and is that act going to come in our spiritual evolution or pull us back?

In summary, I would like to thank the Creator for giving me this opportunity to live life and to feel blessed. I am happy, blessed and content in living my current self, conscious that I am part of a grand design, aware that I possibly need to calm my cravings and desires.

The Secret, 2011

Finally, I request that we seek the knowledge of self and the larger part, be constructive and try to make the world a better place in whatever small shape or form, play our part but keep pivoting to doing good and loving others in this version of the cosmic game that I exist in– *Life 2.0*!

<u>REFERENCES</u>

Hohl, Nate. "Call of Duty: Infinite Warfare Weapons." Opshead. Nate Hohl, 4 May 2016. Web. 11 May 2017.

Chris. "Space Wallpaper Hd Resolution ~ Sdeerwallpaper." Sdeerwallpaper. Sdeer, 12 Aug. 2016. Web. 11 May 2017.

Blake, William. "All Religions Are One." All Religions Are One by William Blake. Glyndw University, 1995. Web. 11 May 2017.

Ostow, Mark. "June 2017." Discover Magazine. Discovermagazine, 10 Oct. 2013. Web. 11 May 2017.

Orancion. "ORACION DIARIA PARA ABUNDANCIA Y PROSPERIDAD ECONOMICA." YouTube. YouTube, 13 Feb. 2016. Web. 11 May 2017.

Khan, Jemal. "Energy Balance." Energy Balance Cayman. Energy Balance Cayman, 2003. Web. 11 May 2017.

"Soul liberty." Soul Liberty. 2011. Accessed

May 11, 2017. http://soulliberty.com/.

"People Are Strange." World News. November 6, 2012. Accessed May 11, 2017. https://wn.com/people_are_strange.

Smithsonian's National Museum of Natural History. Human Family Tree | The Smithsonian Institution's Human Origins Program. March 01, 2010. Accessed May 11, 2017. http://humanorigins.si.edu/evidence/human-family-tree.

"Importance of Science and Technology in National Development – Essay." YourArticleLibrary.com: The Next Generation Library. December 04, 2013. Accessed May 11, 2017. http://www.yourarticlelibrary.com/technology/importance-of-science-and-technology-in-national-development-essay/8563/.

Berg, Vincent. "Touring Under Pressure." Touring Under Pressure (Vincent Berg) - 9781301464418 - Kup książkę. Accessed May 11, 2017. https://pl.diebuchsuche.com/ksiazki-isbn-9781301464418.html.

"HD tapeta na plochu - 3D abstrakce." Návrat na titulní stránku serveru Slunečnice.cz. Accessed May 11, 2017. https://www.slunecnice.cz/sw/hd-tapeta-na-plochu-abstrakce/.

Morrow, Ashley. "Hubble Sees a Star 'Inflating' a Giant Bubble." NASA. April 21, 2016. Accessed May 11, 2017. https://www.nasa.gov/feature/goddard/2016/hubble-sees-a-star-inflating-a-giant-bubble/.

Epstein, Emily Anne. "What Does the Internet Actually Look Like?" The Atlantic. January 05, 2016. Accessed May 11, 2017. https://www.theatlantic.com/technology/archive/2016/01/in-photos-inside-the-internet/422592/.

Slunecnabrana.eu. Accessed May 11, 2017. http://www.slunecnabrana.eu/Slunce/2015/Sun,Cetral%20Sun.htm.

www.ingramcontent.com/pod-product-compliance
Lightning Source LLC
Chambersburg PA
CBHW071530040426
42452CB00008B/948